# TESTIMONY

## from a

# NEW GIRL

*Satan, You Didn't Steal My Joy*

# DIANE HALL

## outskirtspress

DENVER, COLORADO

*Handwritten signatures and inscriptions:*

Lucretia Johnson

Jill

James H. Watt

Travis L. Andrews Jr. 1-31-2014

Bishop Daniel Doyle

Mother McDonald    Mrs. Johnnie ayers

Teyake Tayler

Madeline Andrew

Bishop Charles D Johnson

Sabes que daste Dios

Sandra O. Fano

FIRST I GIVE honor to God and His Son Jesus, and the Holy Spirit that leads and guides me. This book is based on a true story, how I lived by letting seven demons get in control of my life, because I was in love with someone that was not God. But I made him my God, by trying to prove and give to him everything, and I wanted him to know all he needed was me; I wanted him to know that I would do anything for him, and in that I let Satan deceive me, where I didn't let God in. While I was on my journey of destruction, all else followed: the lies, the drugs, the prostitution, and the guilt--and with that came the shame. And these seven demons played major roles in my life--and not only in my life, but they brought pain to the ones that love me. It began with the demon called Unclean. This is my testimony, and it starts like this.

Hi, my name is Unclean. Let me share with you the story of my life, how I came out of a woman, and then got back into here seven times worse. You can read about us in the Bible (Matthew 12:43-45; Romans 1:29-32).

Now in the Bible, Jesus talks about us, but Meany doesn't truly understand how I got back in seven times worse. It all started out with a woman that we call a natural woman, who went through Meany things in life, like drugs, bad men, hatred, jealousy, envy, self-pity, low self-esteem…she was practically filled with every kind of wickedness, including greed, strife, deceit ,malice, boastfulness. She was a God-hater, a gossiper, a murderer and also she was very senseless, faithless, heartless, and ruthless, as well as very disobedient. In the natural woman's mind, she couldn't understand why her heart wanted joy, but her mind kept slanderous thoughts. She didn't know and didn't understand that I, Unclean, kept her house with filthy rags. In her mind is where I live. But one day the natural woman was walking, feeling all depressed, and very much confused, saying to herself, "I'm tired so tired of this life of hurting and hurting others. This life is going nowhere-- no peace, no joy. Help, help!" She cried out, "What shall I do?" God heard her cry, "Have mercy, Lord--I can't do this by myself."

The natural woman heard a voice say, "Jesus is the way the truth and the light; whoever comes to Him shall not perish, but have everlasting life." The natural woman stopped to hear more, because the feeling was so great; it brought joy to her heart and soul. She walked closer and asked the question, "How can I change?"

The man said, "Repent and ask for forgiveness of your sins, and mean it from your heart. And accept Jesus as your Lord and Savior."

The natural woman could feel her heart beating hard, wanting some of this. The man went on to say, "God gives us a choice to choose to do good or to do evil. It is the acceptance of your heart and mind to accept Him to be your personal Savior. Jesus died on the cross for everything that I have gone through; three days later He rose again. He said there had to be the shedding of blood for our sins [Hebrews 9:22] and it was His; He took the final and last suffering to the cross. With everything, which I have faced in this life, all I have to do is give it to Jesus. Jesus loves me, and He said that he could help me."

And the natural woman thought about it, and she remembered Him helping her before, at times in her life when she was struggling, and couldn't keep up. "So what am I supposed to do?" the natural woman asked.

"All you have to do is say the sinner's prayer, and believe that Jesus died for you, and accept Him to be your personal savior. Read the Bible every free moment, to renew your mind."

And the natural woman thought, *if this is all I have to do, then let me try it*. Then he goes on to say, "Get involved in a church and pray unceasingly at all times--pray."

So the natural woman thought about it and accepted Jesus in her heart and started going to church, and oh boy the spirit of Unclean had to leave. He had no choice. Christ and the devil could not and still cannot live together in the same house. So the Unclean spirit roamed through dry places seeking something to feed on, someplace to rest. He found nothing and he was getting bored, so he went back to the house where the woman lived from whom he had come out. The woman's life was empty of sin, but it wasn't filled up yet with the needed things like joy, peace, or contentment of Christ. It had some love, and it had a little joy, but not the life-filling kind that Christ was longing to place there. Something was still dangerously wrong in that house... even when it seemed so right. It was empty of sin, but it was dangerously empty.

So the Unclean spirit went to a convention of demons. He had found no rest outside of the natural woman from whom he had been evicted, but there was still room for him there, he thought, so he went walking around trying to find somebody to use, but he couldn't, because even her friends were Christians. Now it was time to check in, so he tried to sneak in the back door of the convention. As Lucifer stood screaming at the other demons gathered fearfully in front of him, Unclean developed a case of shaky knees. Satan saw him slip in the back door and pointed a flaming finger in his direction. Fiery arrows lunged at the Unclean demon, and he started to quiver.

Lucifer said, "What are you doing here? I thought I sent you to possess Mrs. Natural woman. Give me account of yourself--and it better be good."

By now every leering eye in the room was on Unclean as he answered in a trembling voice, "I was living there until a few days ago, but the natural woman accepted Jesus into her heart and I had to...."

Before he could finish the sentence, Satan shrieked and said, "Don't ever say that name in my presence! I hate it! I hate it! I can't stand to hear it!" As he cried out, the edges of his voice were tinged with fear as the brimstone walls glowed with re-flected fury. Satan said, "You mean you couldn't hold on to her for nothing? You better go back out there and try, because as I can see, she hasn't got too much she's holding on to that will keep you from getting her house. Don't you know I need her and hers?"

So Unclean said, "Okay, I will go."

While Unclean was thinking about how he was going to do this, another demon stood up to address Lucifer. "My name is Discouragement. If you will give me permission to go with Unclean, we will go together to the natural woman and I will help work a few bribes into her to get her discouraged--maybe I'll have another person in church say something negative and nasty about her...you know how some church folk get, always trying to knock the next person because they're not living right, and so they get mad because they know what they're called to

4

do and they're not doing it."

A second demon stood to speak. "My name is Depression. If you let me go with Unclean and Discouragement, just about the time things start going wrong, I'll get her to look at all negative things in her life and get her all depressed...a little extra salt in the wound would do her no harm. It will only keep things at bay,"

A third demon stood. He said, "My name is Defeat. Let me go too--when things are a low point, I'll step in and create a real mess on her job and have one of the employees make it hard for her, and have them always talking to the boss about her and what they feel she isn't doing. If that doesn't work, I'll make the one closest to her agitate her while she's getting ready for church, and then she will get mad, and a grand and glorious argument will get started to where now everything will seem to be out of place, and I'll keep it going till it gets too late to go to church and she might get ready to quit--maybe we can defeat her till she never wants to go back, but gets comfortable in the house watching TV on Sunday."

Excitement was beginning to build, so the fourth demon jumped to his feet and clapped his hands with glee. "My name is Jealousy. When Discouragement, Depression, and Defeat go with Unclean, let me go too, because when the natural woman feels defeated and starts missing church, I'll get her looking at other people instead of at the Word of God--looking at the way people live: having fun, partying, doing things that she thinks are life, and she will start hanging around them because everybody in the church is no better; every time she tries to do something, somebody is always stepping into the position that she wanted in the church, so now her mind is off track for real because now she is even looking at the pastor and how he is always thanking somebody else, but not her for the things she was doing in the church. I'll make her so jealous that she won't ever get over it!"

The fifth demon jumped up with a sneering grin on his face. "My name is Criticism and I want to go too—I'll get her to start criticizing just a little bit with just a little sarcasm thrown in for good measure, and pretty soon she will be attacking everybody and everything that comes around her...you know how decisive women get, and of course I'll make sure some people criticize her on a regular basis. Sauce for the goose is sauce for the gander--you know what I mean. It helps because she will be trying to prove and defend her situation, and she will focus on me."

The sixth demon stood to offer his services. "Don't forget about me--I'm the demon of Judgment. After the natural woman has been overcome by criticism offered about her by others, I'll cause her to start passing judgment on them. I will even make her say that the whole bunch of them are nothing but hypocrites and no good for anything. That ought to go well, and she might give in to me and come home with me and Brother Criticism, if you know what I mean."

And finally a big sour-looking demon pulled himself up; in a hateful, steady, seasoned voice he began to speak. "My name is destruction. This plan of action against the natural woman sounds good to me. I'd like to offer the crowning touch--just as she starts tottering on the brink of the abyss and thinks there might be one last slim chance that she will survive, I'll come in

6

for the kill and finish her off... sort of a last resort for these other six fellows here. You might say I'm the one they save for last."

So they went off to the natural woman, and guess what? Suddenly the house of the natural woman (her life) was full of fury seven times greater than before. Where did it start? How did it happen? It started in an empty corner of the natural woman's mind, with the first thought of Discouragement. It happened step by step and she didn't realize it, because she wasn't watching or directing where those precious drops from God's Words were going…they were going right out the door, so when Unclean, Discouragement, Depression, Defeat, Jealousy, Criticism, and Destruction came, the natural woman gave in by getting careless and allowing herself to go into a comfort zone, and before long her mind was under the sway of Satan's tormenting spirits. Satan's greatest weapon is this kind of camouflage; he remains well-hidden until he is exposed or in control of a person's life. By the time it becomes that obvious, his grip is all the harder to escape.

Now let me tell you how these demons of destruction played a part in my life. This is my testimony of how I let the devil get the best of me and raise me up in a world that I thought had no hope. When I knew God's Word was perfect and had strength and He was always there with me, I let go.

It all started out when I was just a little girl living in a little town called Fresno, California where I was born and raised. I know when I came out of my mother's womb God said, "She belongs to me," and Satan said, "She belongs to me too," because the day I started to walk, Satan showed me how to fear, because that was the first time that I felt I couldn't walk. I fell down, hit the floor, and did not want to get up--but my mother, as happy as she was, just picked me back up and said, "Try it again." I did, and I just kept trying, and one day I just walked all over the house. When I started to talk, I was watching the words that came out of my mother's mouth, and then I started to say the words with her.

Satan couldn't get me to stop walking, so now that I could talk, he taught me to lie. Now I was being disobedient to my mother. I remember my first lie at the age of seven. I asked my mother if I could go outside. She said, "Yes, just don't leave the yard." And what did I do? I left it anyway. You see, we lived in the projects by Edison High School, and I had a friend that I liked to play with all the time. She was about the same age as me, and when she asked me to come over to her house, I did, because she couldn't leave her yard, so I went over to play with her. Back then, Pepsi bottles were made of glass, and we were putting dirt in those bottles, and I was just enjoying myself, thinking about nothing but getting this dirt in the bottle. She got up; now I was bent over with my back toward the ground, and I noticed from the corner of my eye that she went around me. I was still putting dirt in my bottle, enjoying myself, and next thing you know—BAM! I was grabbing my head--I looked up and saw her run into the house. She hit me so hard in the head with that bottle that all I could do was run home.

I was running, crying, "Mama, mama--this girl just hit me upside my head with a bottle!"

My mother grabbed my head and checked it out; she saw I was not bleeding and she asked me, "Where were you?"

Now here came my first lie. I got stuck on stupid because she already told me not to leave the yard and I did anyway, so I lied and said I was by the door and she grabbed me and said, "Show me!"

Man, my heart beat so hard, because you don't lie to Mama--you would just get an extra beating on top of that lie. Mama grabbed me and went outside and I had to show her where I really was, and when I did, she said, "I told you to stay in the yard."

That was my first lie. Thinking about it now, it's crazy how I allowed the girl to ask me to leave the yard and I did, but she didn't leave hers. I was asking for trouble and now that's all I can see…that trouble was calling my name. I was raised in the church; my mother and grandmother made sure that my brothers and sisters and I went to church every Sunday. My grandpa and grandmother would pick us up and it would be my cousins too, so can you just imagine how hot that was on hot days, piled all up on each other, trying to get to Sunday school, but it was a must for my grandmother to get us all to Sunday school, and I'm glad she did.

I liked the stories of David and Goliath and Jonah, how he got swallowed up in the belly of a whale because he disobeyed God. Learning scriptures was my favorite. I learned Psalm 23, which starts "The Lord is my shepherd; I shall not want." I liked that scripture because it gave me assurance that God would be there for me, and that gave me the strength to be strong. I also sang in the choir. I was the one who couldn't keep in tune with everybody else, and that's when Satan taught me how to be discouraged, but I didn't give up--I kept on trying, just keeping up with the others. i was able to learn two songs to sing. One was called "He's able to carry you through," and another was called "Turn it over to Jesus." I enjoyed singing and every time they asked me, even when I couldn't do it the way they felt it should have been done, I got in the spirit and enjoyed myself anyway. One thing I did love to do was sing.

Now let me share with you how school was. I went to a school called Franklin Elementary. I went there from preschool to fourth grade. I remember my first day in kindergarten, waking up early in the morning to that rise and shine and putting on my new clothes. Just knowing I was on my way to walk into a classroom felt good, and when I walked in there it had a smell that made me hungry. When I walked up to my teacher and introduced myself, the smell of graham crackers and peanut butter was so strong it made my stomach growl. It seem like that was the first smell that hit me--I just didn't know where it was coming from until I saw them on the table--and man, I was ready to eat! Every day as I got ready for school, that smell was the one that met me at the door.

I had a beautiful nice teacher, but my classmates, on the other hand, weren't so friendly--they would take anything that I rode on, and if they saw me pick something up, they wanted it. Things got so bad that they didn't even want to play with me-- they just wanted what I had. I always played by myself, and that made me not want to go to school. I felt sad all the time, like I was in a world all by myself. Now I was getting older, but every grade level was about the same--I just graduated on up to grade after grade. PE was a good time for me because I was able to play with the other kids. We played kickball and I would kick that ball real far and run to home base, but getting hit with that ball wasn't the thing, though it stung, and the boys would try to tear your leg off, so I tried to dodge that ball as much as I could. Flag football that was another one of my sports I loved, but as the years went on I got older, and they were passing me up to the next level.

As I grew up I became a tomboy, and I was hanging with my brothers and their friends. My brothers had a treehouse that I used to climb into, and they could not stand when I went up there, but I was nosey and I wanted to know what they were doing up there all day long. I loved climbing trees, so it was my joy to climb up to that treehouse. I liked the view and the things that they had up there. Now stubbornness stepped in and became a part of my life--and in my testimony you will see that these demonic spirits played a role in my life from a very early age. I didn't care what my brothers said; I still went up to that treehouse, and that was a door left open in my life, because when my brothers would tell me to stay out of their things, I just wanted to be a part of their lives…and even when my brothers would go get the big enter tubs and do flips off the house, I was the only girl who would jump off the house, land on the enter tub, and do a flip—and

I wouldn't miss a beat. Now I know that was only God giving me a courageous spirit, I would say, because even the boys wouldn't do it--they thought I was crazy because I would land right on my feet and wouldn't hurt myself.

Growing up for me was tough; I had no friends, but even though my life had its ups and downs and I felt as if I could do anything, I was all alone and living in sadness. Sometimes it felt like I was living in a box and didn't know how to walk or crawl out of it, and it seemed like that was going to be my testimony, because

I went through a lot in life just to get here today, but I see why now--so keep reading; it gets interesting, my testimony.

We have moved out of the projects and moved into a neighborhood, and I started going to another school, called Carver Elementary. The street that we lived on was called Calwa. Every day I would get up to go to school, but it seemed like I couldn't get anything right. My grades was no good and I felt like I was the only kid walking around by myself with no one to play with. It seemed like nobody liked me, because only time I got to play with other kids is when we had to do PE, but through it all I kept on smiling. My teacher would always say, "Diane, I love your smile," and those few words would make my day in spite of everything around me. I just went on as if nothing ever happened.

Back in those days, the principal would paddle you for doing anything wrong. One time I was going to lunch and we had to go through the line first to wash our hands. I was washing my hands, minding my own business, standing there waiting for my turn when all of a sudden this girl just started talking crazy to me. Next thing you know, we were fighting. They broke us up and we were sent to the principal's office. We both got paddled. I still couldn't figure out what I did wrong to her to make her feel like hurting me, but I can see Satan had to teach me to fight to defend myself. But God gave me grace and mercy, and He followed me. The principal told us to hug and say we were sorry. I did, and after that I felt good, as if I had a new friend, and now I could go to school knowing that I was going to be all right, and I didn't have to look over my shoulder anymore. My grades didn't show that I was learning anything at all, but for some reason they just kept promoting me to the next grade.

The neighborhood we lived in had a lot of kids and I got to know them all. My mother did not have much money like the other parents did, but it was okay with me--I didn't care. I just wanted to be a part of their lives. We played cards for candies and built play houses on the side of the fence between the houses, and pretended to have a house to live in, and there was a boy I liked...he was the brother of one of my playmate. I thought he was so cute...when he came around my heart would pound so loud I thought that he could hear it because of the way he would look at me. But as the days went on, getting up for school got hard and long, because now I was in the sixth grade and my grades were still very poor. I was an F student from the time I got to the school, but they just graduated me anyway to the seventh.

I was going to Scandinavian middle school, and what a drag that was--I guess Satan hated me so much that he came along for the ride. On the first day of school I had to go and find where the bus was. I finally found it, and it seemed like Satan found it too, because he was right there every day to call me ugly, stupid, big-nosed...you name it, he claimed it that was me. It seemed like nobody would laugh at or say anything to the person who made fun of me, so I dreaded getting up every day going to school. Two years went by, and I took that abuse-- it was not fun at all. It only kept me in an insecure stage of my life, and how I made it through school, I don't know. I was an F student from the time I got there, and it followed me right to the ninth grade...and Satan did too.

But right now, I'm going to go back and talk about the neighborhood when we lived on Calwa Street, when the enemy just would not stay away from me. He liked picking on me. When they opened up pat tone practice to the kids in the neighborhood, I was one that could not be a part of it because my mother could not afford the things I needed, but it was okay with me, so I just watched every time they had practice because I enjoyed looking at them in their uniforms. But Satan didn't like the fact that I still was smiling, so he would nag at me and make me feel sad. He would make me try to look at what I couldn't do because I didn't have what other kids had--but I had the love of God, and He gave me peace.

I guess the enemy understood that, because when the kids would give parties I would be the only kid in the neighborhood who was not invited, so I would look through my mother's bedroom window at them as they went to the birthday parties. Maybe they knew I couldn't afford a gift--maybe that was what made them not invite me. As I looked out the window and stared at everybody either walking over are getting dropped off, I could hear the music because it was so loud. Everybody was laughing and having fun. I just stood there and watched. I can say a tear or two fell down, but I just held my feelings back and shook it off, and the next day got up like nothing never happened, and still played cards with them when they would let me. Satan had it out for me a long time, but God loved me enough to place a spirit of love--no matter what a person did to me, I smiled and went on.

I was thirteen years of age now. We had moved out of the neighborhood and I was going to a new school now called Edison High. How I got there, I have no clue; I was an F student from day one but I got passed on to the ninth without a care in the world. I tried hard to get better grades, but it seemed like the more I tried, the harder it got--I couldn't understand what I was doing so wrong, and my grades stayed the same...I guess all the sadness of not being loved took a great worth out of me. But I'm here to tell my testimony and show the world you can make it--so keep reading.

Now I lived on a street called Eunice, and I had met new people that I was hanging out with. These girls had known each other for years, and here I came in the picture, a new girl on the block. They were cool, but it's my testimony. At the age of fourteen I got pregnant with my first baby, and I lost it in the toilet I went to use the bathroom and all of a sudden the toilet was red with chunks of stuff in it. I flushed it and cleaned myself up, and I was scared. I was even scared to tell my mom, because I wasn't that close with my mom, and we didn't talk about things like this. My mom had her own problems, and she already didn't like the boy that was coming around the house. So I went to this church that was giving birth control and helping girls that were pregnant. I went over there and told them what had happened, and they told me that I had a miscarriage. I had to be two weeks or less, because it just came out, so I told the one that I got pregnant by. He looked at me held me, and ended up getting pregnant again.

This is where my life with God and Satan really stepped in, even though God was there all the time. I thank God for my mother. She kept me in church, and while I was growing up, she took me to Bible study. She made sure I was with her on Monday nights, and she even made sure I got to choir rehearsal on time. She made sure I was a part of every program they had going on in the church: Christmas programs, Easter programs...we had to learn verses and get up in front of everyone to recite the verse that was given to us. It really was fun. Here is one that I learned to love. It is John 3:16. "For God so loved the world that He gave his only begotten Son, that whosoever believe in Him shall not perish but have everlasting life." What a beautiful scripture.

I thank God for my mother, because what I'm about to talk about is how Satan came in and intervened in my life, and twisted it into what he wanted it to be because of my disobedience to my mother and God. My disobedience gave me no peace in my life growing up, and I wish for no one to have to ride this ride I have taken in my life just to believe…so let me tell you how I met my baby's daddy, the one I turned into my god... the one I placed in front of God Himself. Keep reading.

One day I was roller-skating down the street and I saw this boy. I mean this boy was black and pretty to me, so I started calling him Bowlegs I guess he did not see me like I saw him, so I ended up being with his friend. Every day all of us would meet up at his friend's house and go over there and do things that if my mama knew about she would knock me out for. Bowlegs was going with his friend's sister. All four of us would be in separate places in the room and I would just be kissing my boyfriend, and that's all I would do. I was too scared to do anything else. I was a virgin and I did not like his friend like that.

So one day Bowlegs and my boyfriend came over to the house and we were outside talking. Next thing you know, we got in an argument about something stupid, and now I was out here fighting this dude and Bowlegs was just letting us fight... for what reason, I don't know. He just hauled off and hit me, and that was it. I was hitting this dude like I was a dude myself, until he picked me up and slammed me on the ground. That's when Bowlegs grabbed him off me. I thought, *What*

16

*happened? What did I do to him that was so bad he had the nerve to hit me like this?* He never explained himself, but I did find out later on in life.

Now I was going to Edison High School. I was in the ninth grade, still getting F's in all my classes, and Satan was riding on me, making me feel dumb. All other kids' grades seemed to be fine, and I just didn't know why my grades stayed so low. The teacher didn't come to me to even try to help me understand. I can't see how I got all the way to the ninth grade while getting F's all these years. So I felt dumb.

One day I was walking and here came Bowlegs on a bike. He stopped in front of me, and my heart jumped with happiness because I liked him so very much. He grabbed me, looked at me, and then let me go. I did not see him again until the next day. I was at school in the gym; he came and pushed me to the wall and kissed me. He took away every dumb thought I felt about myself, and made me feel wonderful. He asked me to go steady with him. I was fourteen years old, and I said yes.

The first time I made it out with him, he climbed my mother's spare room window that she uses for company. That's when I got pregnant and lost it, but I did it again sneaking out the window--Satan taught me how to be a creeper. Now I was fourteen and pregnant for real. I had to tell Mama, and I had to let her know who I was pregnant by. My stepdad was not fond of Bowlegs. He saw something I couldn't—he was too fine for me even to want to see anything else. So now here I was telling my mother about this, and she just looked at me and said, "Who is the daddy?" I told her, and yes, she was mad. I was still going to church with my mom. I had to--I was still young and living in her house. I still sang in the choir and was the only one pregnant out of all the girls my age. I still participated in all these church functions even though I was with him, and my mom knew it.

It was hard because I loved my mom and I hated that I disappointed her, but I was in love with Bowlegs. He had a touch that made me feel wanted. He would ask me to go places with him, like to Magic Mountain and I had to ask my mother, because I was still young, and so I would go and ask her if I could go, and she would say no to me, and that made me sad inside--I wanted to be a part of him, and I could see he wanted me there just as bad as I wanted to be there, but I would not argue with my mother. I was young and she was over me because I was nothing but a kid. They would give family parties and I still was in the hoping stage that Momma would say yes--but she would say no, and that brought a lot of confusion into my life. I was in love with this boy, and now Satan was really playing a big role in my life, stabbing me at every turn. When I couldn't go with Bowlegs, he took someone else, but I still smiled and forgave him and her.

As the days went by I was getting bigger and bigger and the church gave me a baby shower. It was so cool--they got together and bought my baby so much...I had so many clothes for my child that I could dress her for a whole month and never wash. Time went on, and the pregnancy went well--it was just the struggles of the other girls that I had to deal with, getting in my face, always trying to fight me over Bowlegs.

My ninth month came along and it was time for me to have my baby. She was a healthy baby girl, Here I was loving my child, feeding her and dressing her, and one day my mom walked in and told me to stop changing the baby's clothes every day; my mother said, "She doesn't need clothes on like that." That took something from me, and Satan knew it would. He would not stop…he wouldn't stay off me. Now it was to the point where the parents couldn't come in and see the baby, and I couldn't even dress my baby the way I wanted to. Now I was mixed up and confused. Satan had taught me how to hurt, and I mean hurt real good. Now Bowlegs was doing his thing—I was in love with him no matter what he did--it did not matter. I gave in and smiled through the storm.

When my baby was a year old, I was pregnant again. By this time, my mama did not make me go to church. She went own her own. Now I was smoking weed, drinking, and ditching school just to be a part of Bowlegs' life. My grades sucked anyway, and I wanted to be free and happy doing things for a change instead of always being let down and told what I couldn't do. All that did was make it worse for me, because now I was dependent on a welfare check for money. There was a time when Bowlegs bought me some clothes for school from the check he had got from his job. He took me shopping and that made me more in love, especially when he brought me a promise ring and showed everybody at school before he showed me… so now people were whispering and looking at me funny and I didn't understand why, until he came up to me and kissed me, and handed me this little box.

"Here," he said, and I smiled. I opened it up and there was a diamond ring with a silver crown. I had so much going on inside me at this time—I didn't know how to respond. I just smiled and said thanks. I had all these emotions running wild in my head and sometimes I didn't know if I was coming or going. I had one baby and was pregnant again; he wasn't doing the right thing and my mama didn't like me right now, but he was all excited.

One day he came to me and asked me to give him some money so he could turn it, and I did, but it did not happen like that. He ended up smoking up the stuff, and I ended up not having diapers because all I tried to do was love him, so I started giving him my checks. He would say, "I'm going to turn it so we can have more," and it seemed never to happen that way. I was left without, but I still smiled and went on loving him--Satan made me feel like he was all I had, so I stood on that. Satan had a way of using Bowlegs to abuse me, because now I was getting slapped upside the head for no reason. I hated it when he would hit me by the Edison day care in front of the other girls. People would lie to him about me and he ate it up, and I got punished for it.

Weed and alcohol had become a part of my life and had gotten intense, but God still was there. I had a healthy baby boy and. He was not messed up from the weed and alcohol that I was taking and abusing. I was out there alone with no one to talk to—I was scared to talk to my mother. So God sent Brother William and his wife, and these where people I used to go to Bible school with, when I was younger. He came to me one day and said the Lord had told him to come find me--and I thank God he did. At that moment I was so high, and I was lost. His wife she looked at me and I could see the concern and compassion she had for me.

He said, "I got a choir I'm putting together--I would love for you to be in it." I was so high; I was feeling kind of funny and stupid, trying to gather myself up, because I couldn't believe that

Brother William was saying this to me right now, and I didn't know how to respond. At this moment I couldn't think, I couldn't talk...I was dumbfounded, but something was tugging at me and I didn't know what to say. But deep down inside I wanted to go. He said, "I'm not leaving till I get an answer." I looked over at Bowlegs, and he told me to go. I went, and I thank God for them—no matter what time of day it was, he came looking for me and would pray over my life, and when I get through with this book, you will see why he had to. Every time he came I was high--but he didn't care, and he wouldn't leave me there. He would said, "I'm not leaving you, so come on...let's go." So every time he came I just went, because I couldn't get high with him standing there.

We never sang anywhere else but at his house. Then one day I got a call that he had fallen out his delivery truck—he worked as a delivery man--and it fell on him and he died, and that deeply affected my life. He and his wife and were my strength. I knew I couldn't let him die in vain. Satan, I see why you hate me-- prayers went out a long time ago, and the man chased me to try to save me, but it was not him--it was God in him.

I was pregnant again with my third child. Bowlegs was the daddy. It did not matter what this man did to me—even if he took my money and spent it on other women he slept with, I still turned the other cheek and let him, and then I let him slap me around. Now he was slapping me on a daily basis, and I smiled like it was nothing. I had two kids and was and pregnant with the third. I was smoking weed, drinking, and doing sherm. I was really mixed up, trying to get high to take away the pain—I was out there in my own place, and doing all this. I wasn't praying; I wasn't reading the Word; and nobody was coming to tell me about the Word of God. The only thing they were saying to me was, "You need to quit; you are only hurting those kids. You aren't going anywhere, and you'll never amount to anything."

Let me remind you—I was in love with Bowlegs. He was all I knew, and I was trying my best to keep a smile on his face. I wanted him to love me. Because I had two kids, now my welfare check was bigger, and he was telling me the same thing: "Let me turn it." So I let him, and now the other women are laughing in my face because he's giving to them what he wouldn't give to me...and then he left me.

I was by myself with two kids and pregnant, and I was on drugs--smoking weed, sherm, and drinking. By this time crack cocaine came into my life and he was out, and now I was doing crack cocaine. The weed habit was still there, but the sherm was gradually leaving the atmosphere, especially when they told me it was embalming fluid that I was smoking, and I said, "Oh, that's why it smelled so bad!" I had always thought it had a very terrible smell, but I just kept on dipping and smoking like it was nothing. But now the high had gone to another level with crack cocaine. It found a home in my life. The embalming fluid was gone and I had a glass pipe in my hand, Now Satan got me really all mixed up and confused. I didn't graduate and I dropped out in the tenth grade, so I had no education, no one to tell me about the Lord, and no one to talk to--only me. I was troubled and lost and very much confused out here in this world, because now my struggle was harder and harder. I loved someone, but I could see that he didn't love me back, and that left a stain inside my heart and mind. But I kept going on, trying to find something that would fill this void.

I didn't understand the fundamentals of this drug; I just smoked it and noticed that it was not like the other drugs…it made you want more. And it played with your emotions real bad to where you would practically do anything for it. I loved my kids and Bowlegs, but that drug had my mind. I just wanted to taste and feel the feeling that it gave. It made me numb--it made me not feel life; it gave me no pain when I smoked it. I didn't have to feel the struggle of being smothered by trying to please some- one. It hid the pain that I was going through. The addiction just of being in love was like a force field that had a hidden agenda to my mind and soul; it gave me what I needed and didn't give me guilt or shame. It hid the very thought of anything that lived alive in me. I just smoked up all the money, and then I smoked up all the things in the house, because now I had sold every- thing I owned. This drug was no joke.

One day, two men came in my house with guns. They put me and my sister on our knees and told us to put our hands behind our heads. We both were pregnant at this time. They put the gun to my head and told Bowlegs, "You better find my drugs or everybody in here is dead, and they will be first." I knew they were not playing, because of who they were, and Bowlegs knew also that this was not a game. He loved us enough to tell them everything, and God gave us a way of escape. After that, my love for Bowlegs was even greater.

Now I was having contractions. It was time to deliver my baby. It was an easy birth--I had no problems having her, but that she was born addicted to crack cocaine. She had crack in her system. I thank God they did not take her from me; they gave me a chance. And she is a strong young women today with no difficulties.

I was eighteen years old and on drugs, and God had been with me through the hard times. He had been giving me grace while Satan just kicked on me like a football in and out of my life, especially at times when I was giving in to Bowlegs' sweet-sounding voice saying, "Baby, I love you." I still wanted him and I wouldn't let anyone else have a part of me. I wanted his love to where my life just played a cycle around him, and my kids had to suffer. Now I was on this mind-bending drug called crack cocaine, and young with three kids and pregnant. I had two girls and a boy and I was on welfare. Now I was living with my grandfather. I wasn't doing sherm or marijuana, but I was smoking the heck out of that crack pipe, addicted and needing it just to get through, and using all my money to get more. My kids didn't have food, and I couldn't see straight.

I wanted so badly to change—I was tired of seeing my babies going without. One day my little girl knocked on my door while I was getting high and said, "Stop that! Stop that!" But did I stop? No. I kept on smoking and kicking back with Bowlegs, doing things that he couldn't even feel, I was like a dog in the room doing nothing for him, because he was not satisfied with me, though I tried hard to love him.

I was at grandfather's house, but I did not have to go too far to get drugs because they was always sold around me, my uncle was a dealer, and all I had to do was wait until he came over. Are my peeps sold it, I just had to wait until he woke up, and he was right in the same house, so crack was always right there with me. One day at my grandfather's house, I thought about stopping. I wanted to stop smoking--I was tired of living like this. So I got up that morning after thinking about it all night long, trying to figure out how I was going to do this. I said,

"I'll start by cleaning up my grandfather's house, buying things with my money to fix it up." I was looking forward to this, so I said, "I'll start in the morning." The Lord let me wake up that morning, and I still was ready for my change--no doubt I was tired. I had to stop somehow...three kids, pregnant and alone. "Man, I got to do something," I said. When my eyes opened up, I thanked the Lord for another day. I started folding my clothes and next thing I knew my door was pushed open and I was getting hollered at.

"Get up!" she said. "Get yo black bla bla bla up!" I was standing there looking at her; I was already up. She said, "Get up and get out of this house."

My three kids looked up at me, and I grabbed them. They were small children--my oldest had to be about seven. I was pregnant with my fourth child, and I was looking at this woman, and she was telling me to get out, so I grabbed my kids and next thing you know, they were hitting me with their fists. My grandfather was hitting me with an apple juice bottle in the back of my head and back; I had my kids in front of me and I was holding my stomach with one hand with my kids under me, pushing them out the door. I was eight months pregnant and my mother didn't know any better; she was standing there watching the controller control.

I finally made it outside. We had a park called High Hill Park, so I took my kids up there because I had to think--I was crying and hurting because I could not believe this just happened to me. Next thing you know, CPS was at the house and they took my kids away from me. That was when CPS became part of my life. Thank God for my mother--she took my kids. I had nowhere to stay because my aunt would not let me stay with my grandfather, so my mom went on ahead and let me stay with her. I was eight months pregnant, with no income, and now I was dependent on drugs. I was lonely; I was by myself no one to talk to, in love with somebody who couldn't even feel me or talk to me, and now I had to put something together because I could not be there with my kids. They were in the system now, and if I didn't do something soon, CPS would take them from my mom, and I did not want that to happen.

Every morning at seven I had to leave my mom's house. The only place I had to go was back to my grandpa's house. I had nowhere else to go. Every day that went by, I thought about my baby that I still had in me, so I got strong within and I said, "I'll sell joints since I don't smoke weed, and crack since I don't smoke that much." I did, and I stacked my money up every day. I didn't tell anybody about it, and I hid it up under the mattress. As I came home every night, I was getting close to having my baby, and I knew it. In the midst of my storm, Satan thought he won--but God stepped in, and He let me save some money. I knew that my mother did not have money; she was barely getting by with my other kids, and I couldn't help her because she would not accept drug money from me, and I knew it.

It was time to have my baby. My birth pains were starting now, and I was timing them, so I went to wake my mother up. She called my other auntie to go with her--mind you, the pains were coming. I was dilated seven centimeters. The train was coming! My mother pushed on the gas pedal, and she got over the train tracks. We made it to the hospital, and in less than an hour, my baby was here a little girl. I looked at my mother's face; I could see she was worried because she had no money and the baby needed things.

The next day when my mom came to see me, I told her to look under my mattress and go shopping. I had put away a thousand dollars without her knowing it, and you should have seen my mother's face--she had a ball, she and my auntie, and that was God, because he saw my heart had change in it. By the way, I know that day the devil got mad because he knew he was losing me, so he had to send his demon of disturbance my way. But I still won. But that was not the last of the crack mission--my baby came out with drugs in her system and they took her, I had to go through some classes to get my children back. I went through them, but I did not stop smoking on that crack cocaine. Taking the classes gave me rights to see my children, but it took being clean to get them back. I went through the programs, but it was hard--I was still confused, still on drugs, and still in love with Bowlegs...and he was still using. Now let me tell you--I loved my kids, and I wanted to do right, but it was hard not having anywhere to stay, so things for me were hard, just running from place to place trying to understand myself. I had no place to go; my mother would always make me leave the house.

So now I was out in the world with no education, and on drugs. I went to my cousin's house. I was on drugs and had no money...and guess who walked through the door? It was Bowlegs, holding hands with someone else. He had money, a car, dope, alcohol, and he was kicking it. I had to wonder why, and I was hurting deep with jealousy and envy, holding on to my composure, saying nothing to either of them. I didn't know what I'd done to him to be treated like this. I was thinking about my kids and the situation they were in, not having me, and I just wanted to go to sleep. So I went and got on the couch and lay down, and there was a guy there who wouldn't stop looking at me. I told him to move, and to quit looking at me. My sister heard what was happening, and she grabbed a machete and pulled it on him, telling him to leave me alone. "Get away from her!" she screamed. I was just tired of him staring at me, but when she pulled that machete out, I knew she was capable of anything, and I saw the devil—he was just waiting for a freak accident because he didn't win in the situation. When Bowlegs came through the door, I should have been trying to kill him, but I wasn't—so Satan, you got made.

I grabbed him by the hand and said, "Let's go," because now that I was up, I wanted crack, and I had to go find it--my body was craving it--so we left, and I ended up taking somebody's money from with the thought that I was going to date him. Now we were on our way to buy some crack, and I was hurting inside with misery because I was stuck out here in a world with someone I didn't want, and my kids were gone, and Bowlegs was kicking back having the time of his life without me. I said, "Forget it," and kicked it with my new baby daddy, because that one time I ended up pregnant and here I was going to jail for selling crack cocaine. It was my third strike, and this time they were coming down hard, trying to prove a point. The other two times happened at my grandfather's house. Every time, I had sold to an undercover cop.

Now I was pregnant again, but I had no clue who the father was. I thought, *I really know Bowlegs will not want me now.* I loved Bowlegs; he was like my world. I was a virgin when I met him and he was all I knew; even though he was not there, my mind kept him there.

I was locked up. My mama got my kids and now I was suffering from the stain that was within me, and my kids didn't have their mama or daddy in their lives. I was crying to myself, *how do I get away from this pressure of life that I have built inside of me?* The humiliation of going to jail is awful; you have to wait and wait for your name to be called, and then you have to take your clothes off, and while you are naked they tell you to bend over and cough. I hated that part.

When I went to jail, I told myself, "This has got to stop somehow." I was tired, hungry, and worn out from being out there in the streets dragging myself, when I went upstairs I instantly went to sleep. The next day one of the girls came and told me about a woman who held church inside the cells, so I went. It's funny that I waited until I got in trouble before I looked for God. I went, and everything that I was taught was given to me. She told me how God loves me and how He has forgiven me from my sins. She told me that I could start all over again if I just believed, and tears just rolled off my face and I accepted God in my life. She told me everything would be okay, and I believed her. She handed me a Bible and I started reading the Word, and as I read I could see how the Holy Spirit joined in. As I talked to God, tears just rolled off my face, and from that day I thanked God for bringing me here, because now I had a chance to start all over again. She said that His mercy is new every day.

Now I had a new understanding in my life and some peace about me, and I prayed to the Lord and asked Him to help me because I could not do it on my own. I did six months in jail because of going back and forth to court. Finally they sentenced me, and at that time they were trying to make a point about that "three strikes" rule, I and I got caught up in that, so they sentenced me to ten years and I went to C.I.W prison for women.

I don't think my mother even understood my sentence. When I got there, they couldn't find my paperwork, so instead of making themselves look like fools, they sent me to C.R.C. prison and gave me four months. So altogether, I did a year. I had my baby in prison, a beautiful little girl, I gave her my last name; I knew nothing about the man who was her father, and she was not Bowlegs' daughter, so what else was I supposed to do? I thank God for my mother and my auntie. They got on a bus and came and got my child for me.

During the time that I was in prison, I was reading the Word and going to church; I was feeding myself with the Spirit, because I knew that was the only way to survive. So as I did my time I kept my mind on my new journey, because now I had five kids--four girls and a boy--and here I was, sitting in prison. I missed my kids and I missed Mr. Bowlegs. I loved that man so much, and I knew that in order for him to love me I had to prove myself strong.

My time was coming up to go home, and a week before I could even get out the door, here came Satan. But now I was prayed up—I had the Word in me, so now I had Jesus, because it was Him that allowed me to get through all this, especially with the women who cussed me out because I would not turn. I'm a woman, and I love men, and the Word taught me it was wrong. Well, I had my whole armor on, and I thank God I had it on this day, because this girl slammed my locker, got in my face, and called me names that I could have just beaten her for, but the Lord sustained me. I just stood there and let her, because I knew that the devil did not want me to come home. If I had defended myself, thirty more days would have been added to my pain, and I did not need that, so I apologized to her. She walked away mad--but hey, I won. You see, I knew the Word. I carried Psalm 23 in my heart, as well as Isaiah 54:17, which says, "No weapon formed against me shall prosper, for I am more than a conqueror in Jesus Christ that strengthens me."

God allowed me to leave that prison. They had a saying: "Don't look back at the prison when you leave," and in my heart, after all the humiliation I went through, starting from the jail, I knew I never wanted to see prison again. I got out and I went and stayed with my mother

I was on parole, and at this time I still did not have my kids. I had to get involved in a program, so I did an outside program, with AA meetings child care classes, and I was going to church. I got linked up with a Christian woman who helped women coming out of prison to keep their minds on God, and she kept in touch with me, picking me up and taking me to church. She helped by giving me a foundation in the Word, because the Word was the only thing that sustained me against the enemy.

I was still seeing Bowlegs and my parole officer told me one day that I would never change--that I was going to stay on parole forever because I was still seeing Bowlegs, and he felt he was the source of my trouble. Well, I fooled that parole officer. I focused on all the things that had me messed up, and got off parole. I got my kids back, and I was doing well. I had been off drugs for two years: one year in prison, and one on the streets, and as long as I was going to church, things in my life were going fine.

However, I let trouble and loneliness get me drinking again, and I started hanging around some old friends because I wanted Bowlegs so bad, and did not want to accept that he didn't want me. He was treating me so harshly, and I was so sad inside because I was raising my five kids alone, holding up under pressure from my family...and then I got pregnant with my sixth child. Yes, Bowlegs was the father. He was the love of my life. I adored him, and loved him with a love that took full control of my life. It didn't matter what he did to me; I just overlooked it and loved him anyway. I accepted everything he dished out, because I made him my god.

Now I was drinking hard liquor because of the pain that is in me from loving Bowlegs and wanting him to love me back. This feeling that was going on inside of me was taking control of me to the point where I couldn't see what was going on around me--and to top it off, it seemed like my family was not letting up on me. I started partying, going to the club and drinking. I partied from Sunday back to Sunday, seven days a week. I was having fun dancing in the clubs, and that kept my mind off my problems. I met a new man who was sweet to the bone and good for my soul, and I was having fun with him. He looked good to me, and he liked me. I was digging him, so now I had a dancing partner, and I was really looking forward to going to the club. Bowlegs hadn't changed, and I didn't want any part of that life anymore, with the drugs. I was fine, just partying, and I didn't want another drug-addicted baby.

My new partner knew I was pregnant, but he did not care. We kicked it every chance we got. He brought joy where the joy had left, where the pain got in from being young, dumb, and lonely. God gave him to me--at least, that's what I felt--so he could help me stay strong.

The time came to have my baby. I had a son. Now I had four girls and two boys. I was living my life on alcohol and partying in the club, and Satan was playing me. I had now become a real alcoholic and when I say that, I mean I slept with a bottle under my pillow, and when I opened my eyes, my bottle had to be there. It seemed like that was the only thing that gave me happiness. Yes, I still had God in my mind, but I did not have Him in my heart like I did when I first got out of prison. I was trying to live, and looking at the problem I faced of still wanting Bowlegs to help and be part of these children's lives and mine, but I guess he could not love me because of the lies that people told him about me. When I had a child that wasn't his, that really took a toll on our relationship. The kisses that he had stopped giving me long ago became the hugs that I would never feel, but I just overlooked it and accepted it all. At the same time, he would never get out of my life completely, and I would not leave him no matter what went on.

One day he asked me to marry him. He said if I loved him, I would marry him, and I did…and I married not only him, but also the demons that were in him. Those demons knew my love for him was greater than my love for God, and they used that against me. Now I was out of the Word and wanting to get back into it, but I didn't know how. I was lost and out of control because my major obsession was alcohol, to fill the empty void that surrounded me with sadness. I had my own place now and I was still drinking and partying and giving big parties. My kids were still young, and my dad was living with me now. It was a good feeling to have my dad around, because he came at a time in my life when I needed him, and he needed me. He was able to be a babysitter for me, and I was able to take care of him, because he had cancer.

My life was going back around in a circle, and I did not see it. Satan knew, though. I got blindsided—I didn't see it coming. I was taking care of my dad, still partying and drinking; Bowlegs was doing his thing. I fell in love with my club partner, and my kids were suffering because their mama was all mixed up, and tore up from the floor up, as they say. It was like I had a blindfold on.

My daddy left and went back home to Oklahoma City, and that's where he died two weeks later. Things got tough for me. Here I was, pregnant again, and now I was smoking weed and drinking. I didn't know who was the father of the baby, Bowlegs or my club partner. I was loving on both of them. My partner kept me strong; Bowlegs kept me weak. I told Bowlegs about my partner. I said I loved him--and wow, that took a control over my life. It turned out that crack was not my worst nightmare…Bowlegs was. I finally had the baby, and when she came I knew who she belonged to--it was obvious. Bowlegs claimed her as his own.

I moved out of my spot and moved into my brother's house because somebody needed to watch his house while he was away, so I decided to move in and I walked away from my spot to his, thinking that that would help save me some money. His house was paid for--that meant no rent, only utilities. I was living in my brother's house, smoking weed and drinking. Bowlegs was doing his thing, and my partner was still around, helping me to keep my head above water. He did not like it that I did drugs, so he would come around just to help keep my mind off them—he knew I wouldn't do drugs around him, and that became my strength.

But one day I hit that pipe again and I gave in to it, and I did not stop. As a matter of fact, it was even worse than before. I was using all my money just to get high, and still believing that Bowlegs would make more money for me, like he kept saying, so I gave him my welfare checks, thinking things would get better. But as usual, this just kept the kids from eating and having the things they needed, so I was dependent on my mother for food. The unpaid utility bills were piling up, and my brother was getting ready to come home. I was on drugs, and the house was a mess…and where would I go now? My mother did not want me and my seven kids at her house, so guess what? CPS got in the mix again.

I lost everything again. In order to get my kids back, I had to get through a drug program. Four of my children went to my mom's house, one went to my auntie's house, and two went to a foster family I didn't know at all. I was troubled and scared and still alone with no one to talk to, and no one to tell me how to get out of this situation. I went into a program that my CPS worker introduced me to, and it turned out to be a godly program.

Knowing that two of my kids were not with family tortured me way deep down inside. I can still feel that pain today as I write and tell my testimony of how God was always with me, but the devil kept torturing me. He had me in a place that gave me no sight; he showed me how to only look at my feelings, and I know now that feelings are confusing to the mind, because when I look at my feelings, I am looking only at what is going on around me, and I'm not able to see outside myself to what is really going on. So when I was living that way, my world was dark and cloudy.

I was in this program learning about the Word again, getting to know who the Father is, singing and learning of the warfare and strongholds that kept me in bondage. I got visiting rights to see my children, so I could go to my mom's house and visit my children. The social worker brought the other two to see me, and on the first visit I had with them, my youngest son said, "Why do we have to be over there? Why can't we be here with everybody else?" My heart fell into my stomach at this point, because this was my son, the one my family couldn't get. His big beautiful eyes glowed at me with sadness. I looked over at my daughter's head, and it was so nappy, and both of them were ashy, and there was nothing I could say or do. I cried right there for me and everybody else, because I did that--I placed them in that position. I made them feel left out because of my decisions, so I ran with that thought, and I got myself together. I did everything the judge said to do. It was not easy, living in a house full of women and trying to stay strong and out of trouble, but I did, because the sound of my son's voice penetrated me with a sharpness that I could not bear. It haunted me, the very thought of my kids being separated.

I went in that courtroom with confidence. I was reading my Word and the Lord was talking to me, letting me know (Luke 12:31) "seek ye first the kingdom of God and all things will be added to you." I stepped in that courtroom and I saw angels in every corner. I was not worried about my tomorrow; I knew that God had it in control. I trusted Him and His Word. (Romans 8:28) He said all things work together for the good of those who trust in the Lord and. The judge looked at me and said, "Next month you shall have the two little ones with you in the home, so get ready, and we will give you a child every month till they're all there all at home with you."

Let me tell you, God is awesome. He gave me a social worker who saw my heart. She dug deep and did not judge me from where I was or where I came from. I prepared myself and my room for my kids to come, and the day they brought them to me was the best relief in my life. We had fun, me and my little ones, and every week we went and visited my other children. I looked at my kids and said, "Hold on a little while longer; Mama is coming to get y'all too."

One day I was in the kitchen cleaning up at the home, and the Lord showed me one day I would be washing off my own counter, and that's when I started saving my own money and began buying things like dishes. I was putting them under my bed, and the other girls thought I was crazy, but I knew God had a plan for my life. I knew that things was going to get better for me, and they did. I moved in my own place, and each month God gave me a kid. From the youngest to the oldest, it took five months to get them all, and it was exciting for me. I stayed clean, I stayed in the Word, and I stayed in church.

My Auntie moved out of her house just to move into the apartment next to me—I love her so much, and if she were alive today, she would see that all her prayers were not in vain. She said to me I could live anywhere I chose to, but the Lord was asking her to follow me. It was true that I was still in love with Bowlegs, and she knew it. She also knew that the devil was going to ride me with every ounce he had. He did not like how I believed and trusted in God. The other girls started to believe, and God worked in their lives as well, so my auntie started having Bible study in her apartment so that we would stay in the Word. There were a lot of us going through something, and I thank God for it.

One day Bowlegs had given me some money to buy things for the apartment. He was coming to stay with me. The kids loved their daddy, and so did I. CPS was not in my life anymore, so it was okay for him to come around. I was getting ready to take a shower, and I left one of my girlfriends in the house, trying to show her that I trusted her. I got out of the shower, and she was gone...and guess what? My money was gone, too. I was upset and angry, and ready to kill this girl. I went crying to my aunt because I was trying to live for God, and I was doing good. This girl was pregnant, and I didn't want to lose my kids by going back to prison if I took it out on her like I wanted to, so I prayed and sucked it up, but it hurt so bad. I looked at my kids every day and said, "She isn't worth it."

To add fuel to the fire, Bowlegs told me he was glad it happened. As usual, I sucked it up and overlooked it, and still loved him, and went on. I was always kicking him out of the house because I was afraid that I would fall back into using drugs. He was still choosing that lifestyle, so it was crazy for me to be in love with him, still trying to live right. It was hard for me with everybody wanting to fight me or talk crazy to me for some reason, but I stayed strong, and Auntie was right there to let me cry on her shoulder.

One day these girls got in my face, telling me, "I'm not sleeping with your man," and that wasn't the first time I'd had this problem. I'd had to fight girls while I was pregnant, and Bowlegs stood right there and watched his baby mama get beaten up, even by family members. I had to fight to keep them from taking the money. My brother gave me a gun one time because females would just show up at my house for no apparent reason just to fight me. I never could understand it then, but I do today. I got out with the prayers of my auntie, just telling me to hold on. She said Satan didn't like me because I was living right and wasn't hurting anybody anymore. Every time I got back on the drugs, it took a toll on my mother's life. She always worried about her children, but I stayed strong through it all, and I was off drugs for a long time--no drinking, no smoking, just me and the Lord.

One day Bowlegs came home from work and said, "I found a house. The man said we can move in without the deposit if we just give him the first month's rent." Yes, we moved…and Satan moved in too. It was a beautiful home. I really loved it and so did my kids. Now I was far from my auntie, but still in the Word. She always called me and would make sure I was reading my Bible. She kept checking up on me. She had to ride this river with me, so she knew the Word would help me.

I had got my kids and my nieces together, and started a praise team. My cousin and I started going to her church, and that kept me in the Word. Bowlegs and I got a business of our own cleaning houses, and we ended up with a car, so we cleaned houses and threw the newspaper every morning, and he was there for me and my love for him was great, but then he started not caring again. This is where my love for him was greater than the love for myself. I was struggling to get the kids to school and go throw the newspaper by myself. I didn't believe in just letting go and walking off; I wanted to give my notice. Now I wasn't reading the word or going to church. I fell off and now I was back on crack cocaine, although I'd been off drugs for four years. I was messed up. I used to have Bible study in my home—I was in it to win it, and I let Satan throw me off balance because I wanted to be part of Bowlegs' life. I desired him like I desired water, and

Satan used that against me by putting frustrating obstacles and weariness in front of me.

Here I was trying to raise these kids on my own, which wasn't hard--I had beautiful kids; they gave me no problem even when they were going through this with me. My kids have their own story to tell someday. I was back on the drugs with the devil himself—in Satan's den, kicking it with the imps, getting high. I couldn't pay my rent, I couldn't clean houses, and I couldn't throw the newspaper. I had to move out. I had been doing well, but I let myself down, and I was messed up, feeling guilty and scared and ashamed. I was on drugs, feeling like a fool, trying to act presentable while my body was craving Bowlegs and crack.

We went out and found a place to move that based approvals on income rather than a deposit. The Lord gave me a place in the back that was near a Christian woman. People said she wasn't right, and that she was mean. I didn't know anybody and didn't care to know anybody; I was on drugs, and ashamed of myself. My kids were angry, and they had the right to be. They should not have had to be at the mercy of my stupidity again. Here i was again, doing something that made no sence. I was as miserable as ever, and Bowlegs wasn't there. He took the dope and the money, and was kicking it with someone else. I was alone, cracked-out, and had just gotten started again with this mess. I hadn't been on it long, and I was stupid.

One day we were kicking it and he left, telling me he would be back. I went into the bathroom and saw some crack he left. I smoked it, not knowing that it would almost kill me. My body was craving, trying to push down the pain that I had caused in my family and in myself. Bowlegs told me that he would be right back, but I had been through that a thousand times. After I smoked the crack, I didn't have any more, so I went to sleep. I was scared of the streets--I knew nothing about what it was like out there. He came home later that night. I was asleep. Next thing you know, I was getting feverish, and then my taste buds left, and then I couldn't smell…and now my eyes were getting blurry. I took some pain pills, hoping the fever would go away, but it got higher. I lay there on that couch for two whole days. Everything that I smelled stank to me. I couldn't eat; I had no appetite, and I was not hungry, so I went into a deep sleep, and I had a dream.

In my dream I was lying on the bed and I was looking up and I saw a person in a white robe. As I looked down I saw a person, a man—big, natural, beautiful, and brown…I mean that the man was beautiful to me. He kept saying, "Come with me," and the one in the white robe would say, "No, don't go," and I would look down at the man who was telling me to come with him. He was the most beautiful thing you could ever want to see, but the one in the white robe kept insisting, "No, don't go." I woke up and told my oldest daughter get me to the hospital.

When I got there, I saw a doctor called Dr. Brown. He said, "How are you doing?" and I told him what was going on. When I got there, they took my temperature, which was 103, and I hadn't been able to make it go down at all. He told me that I had just barely made it—if I had stayed on that couch any longer, I would have died. My kidneys were shutting down. What had happened was that the drug set off a reaction that was killing the cells inside of me, but I thought it was just a cold. He put me on antibiotics for seven days, and when one bottle was empty, they gave me another. For the next three days I was eating, and

I could hear and smell. My eyes were doing better, and the fever was going away. My kidneys got better, and my heart got stronger. I told the doctor the truth about what had happened, and I believe that because I told the truth, God had pity on me. I didn't remember this doctor at the time, but I do today--he delivered one of my kids. I thank God he had a Christ-like love in him, because he saved my life.

I got out of the hospital after being in there for seven days, and I felt good. I wasn't craving, and God had given me another chance to live. I was ready to go all the way with God, so I started cleaning up the house. As I was cleaning up, I got to my son's room, and when I cleaned out his dresser drawer, guess what I found? A bag of crack cocaine. I looked at it, and I had to make up my mind right there--I could either smoke it, or give it away. I told myself, "God has brought me out of the lion's den, and I'm going to take it." I told Satan, "You are a liar," and he whispered in my ear, "Give it to your brother--go sell it to him." I told Satan, "You are a liar still." I couldn't see myself helping the enemy destroy someone else's life, so I put the crack down the drain in front of my apartment and said, "Lord, it's done--no more."

My son called my daughter and asked her, "Is Mama high?"

She said, "No, Mama is fine. She is singing and cleaning up the house. I've been watching her all day. Mama's doing good."

My son came home and said, "Mama, what did you do with that bag of rocks?"

I said, "I put it down the drain outside."

He was mad at me, but he was happier that I did not smoke it, and from this day my son has been over blessed. He owed somebody for that bag, but he did not let it take him there; he held on. And Mama got strong. I was only on those drugs three weeks, and I had not finished packing--but I realized that I needed to get in the Word, so I started going to my home church, and all of a sudden my truck broke down. I couldn't go to my home church, and I was thinking to myself that I had to get into somebody's church, so I went to the church in my building. They had just gotten started in ministry. I stayed under the leadership of that pastor, and I got my kids together, and we got all the kids in the neighborhood and built a praise team. We put on Christmas programs with the pastor. The pastor had a vision, and a big one--he loved people, and my children and I stayed under his anointing for seven years…until one day I was told that it was time for me to leave.

Now I was lost again, with no church home, and all my family lost their church, too. What happened was that the pastor chose Bowlegs over me. You see, Bowlegs started going to church with me and the kids, and we were one big family. The kids and I were involved in everything that was going on in the church, and so was Bowlegs, but one day I got tired off Bowlegs cheating with the other females in the church, acting as if I was not his wife. I started complaining to the pastor about this matter because this pain that I was feeling was not healthy. I couldn't think my prayers were empty, but I had to keep going because of my children and my family members who had just gotten started.

I talked to my husband about it and he just denied it, so I took it to the pastor. He had a lot going on at this point; he had just opened up a home for men and he needed Bowlegs. I was so angry, and I did not know how to handle this--I had been with the church with my kids for so many years; it wasn't fair that I should have to face this kind of torture. I did not know what to do. I was getting lied on, and that did not bother me, but I did have a problem with it when Bowlegs was cheating with women in the church and they were walking around smiling in my face, as if this was cool.

I went to the pastor again and he said, "I think it's time for you to leave." My heart fell right to the floor--I could not believe this just came out of his mouth. I had served this church for seven years. I didn't know where my children and I would go, not to mention the rest of the family who had come with me to this church. I hung up the phone and just cried, because I couldn't believe this. I needed God. I knew what it was like not to have Him a part of my life--there was room for the enemy, and now I was feeling lost. I didn't know anything but this ministry, and I loved helping this pastor. He showed things to me and my kids; he brought the power of God's love to us. My kids were look-ing at me as if to say, "Mama, what now?" I did not give up--I prayed, and I talked to God, and I asked God for forgiveness for whatever I did. I even asked Bowlegs and the pastor and the church for forgiveness, with a letter, because the Bible had taught me to forgive so God can forgive me.

Well, the Lord let me see another Sunday. I got up to find a church, and I cried all the way as I was riding around looking for one to go to. I did not know what to do, because I needed a church that my children and I could work in, because that was all we knew to do...to work in the Lord's kingdom. We loved helping. As I was riding around, I was looking at these churches and not feeling them, so I went to my mother's house and cried on her shoulder because I knew that without a hedge, there is room for the devil. My mother comforted me--and yes, she was upset, because she knew how the devil plays his tricks.

The next Sunday, I went back to my home church, and after the hostility I encountered there, I dared not go back. It wasn't right that my children should be the subject of criticism because they didn't have Sunday clothes. I had no money, and where we came from, that wasn't an issue for us.

Another Sunday came around. I saw a sister in Christ and she told me about a church she was going to. I went with her, and now I was doing well under the umbrella of the covenant of God again, loving the Lord and all that is involved in loving the Lord. My kids and I were reading the Word, but I still felt empty. I didn't have a vision, and felt like I wasn't growing. I didn't stop going to church, but now I was drinking and having parties, from birthday parties to weddings. My reading of the Word slowed down. I was happy, but I was empty.

Bowlegs came and went, and I was thinking about kicking him out for good because I didn't want to go back on crack. I was afraid to lose what I had…that's how I fell back down in the first place: no covering, and no hedge. I was loving my family and my kids, but now I was going to the casino and spending all my money. My addiction went from crack cocaine to gambling, and now I wasn't in the Word, and I wasn't in a church.

I took all my attention and placed in on the machine. It got so bad that gambling felt like a drug. I was addicted to the sound of the machine getting happy when I would get a bonus, and couldn't wait to get back just to play the machines on Fridays.

So now I had another addiction, though I was trying to find happiness. I couldn't find it in my kids or in my partner, and I couldn't find it in my family. It seemed like everything I tried to do took something out of me that wasn't right. I was empty and sad, and frustrated to the bone.

By now, I had grandchildren, and I was still trying to hold out, still trying to do the right thing. I was making pillows and selling them, and I had a good job working in child care. I had a client with in home supportive service, and I was surviving. I was still with the church and involved in the ministry, but things were not quit right in me. The pastor and his wife would show up to see why I was missing church, and I did not have a real answer for them. I would just say, "I'll be back."

I was empty, and all I wanted was to smile, so on New Years of 2010, I hit the crack pipe...and boy, was that a curse. I was drinking and Bowlegs was doing his thing in the bathroom. I walked in and I looked at him and said, "Let me hit that." He let me...what a mistake. I felt so stupid, but I wanted more. We got high. The kids didn't know it yet. At this time all the kids were home except for my oldest son, who had his own place at this time. I had money because the kids were paying rent to me, and I had money from my job, and it was income tax time. So here I was getting high on crack cocaine, and loving it...because I was kicking it with Bowlegs, and we were doing what couples do, and he was loving me. But through it all, I was smoking this crack pipe. I knew my pipe should be full, but it wasn't, so I knew I needed some more drugs.

Now I had to spend some money. The dope kept disappearing. Now I was depressed, spending money on drugs and cigarettes, smoking like a <u>train</u>. My nerves were messed up, and my kids couldn't understand why this was happening. I had been clean for ten years—why did I go back to it. I told them, "Y'all don't understand," but inside, I couldn't understand it either.

You see, things looked good. I lived in a house where my room was upstairs, like it was a separate apartment. I had everything: a big screen TV, computers…anything a woman would need, I had, but what I didn't have was a covering over my mind because I still wanted Bowlegs no matter what. When I got high, we went to places he knew of and spent time around girls that he used my money on. He thought that I didn't see him giving them crack and money. I noticed, but I just overlooked it, as always. I was tired of arguing. Every time I said something, they acted like I was crazy, but I saw it and kept on going. I felt like a queen up under him because I would do things to make them mad, and he knew, so he would tell me to stop. He took me to places where he had planted a seed of affection toward people, and I was just the income to keep him and them happy. I was only a source, a provider…I was being used.

One day he asked me to do a threesome with him, and I thought, *what the hell…if it makes him happy, that's fine.* All I wanted was for him to be happy and forget about what it would take to make me happy, and Satan knew that. Satan has hated me for a long time, and I can see why. This particular day, we went and picked the girl up. By now, my kids had found their own places, and I had to move, too. I couldn't afford rent or utilities, and things got tough.

Anyway we went to go get her. We went into my room and started to play a card game. The next thing I knew, I woke up lying on the couch at the foot of my bed. I was dizzy, and I didn't know how I had ended up there. I was trying to get my thoughts together, but I had no memory of that night. I went and looked in the bathroom and saw my computer desk chair. I could tell that Bowlegs and the girl had kicked it in there. As I got up, I was trying to remember how I got here and trying to figure out where Bowlegs was. I looked out my bedroom window, and I saw my truck was gone. I tried to go downstairs, but I fell, and started sliding down the stairs. I crawled to the phone to call him and tell him I could hardly breathe or walk.

In just a few minutes, I smelled rubber and heard screeching tires. It was Bowlegs in my truck, and he was flying. He looked at me and grabbed me with a hug, and said, "Thank God!" I thank God that I woke up; I should have been dead. It was by the grace of God I woke up that day, because my drink was spiked with sleeping pills and eye drops to get me out the picture. I was still smoking and tripping, so I let it go, just like always.

Now I had to move, and there wasn't anything to do except go back to my brother's house. Anybody and everybody did whatever they wanted in that house, and Bowlegs already knew all the people at my brother's house. But I was new to them, and they were new to me, and the devil was there too, because I did not understand how close these people were to Satan. This opened up a cage of ancient demons that worked on me until I was living in a nightmare. I called them the demons of darkness. What they do is use people, especially those who don't understand what's out there. You see, it was as if I was new to the game of crack cocaine, because I was off drugs for ten years. The demons out there were nothing like the church people who didn't want to live right. The demons just hated me…they hated me so much that they did whatever they could to show it. I lost my place and had to get rid of everything that was in my house. This was not the first time in my life that I'd lost everything, but I knew I'd caused this, and I have accepted that fact.

I sold everything that the kids and I didn't want, and then I put everything else in my truck—clothes, makeup, jewelry… you name it, it was in that truck, because there were a lot of people living at my brother's house, so I just gradually changed clothes using the trunk of my truck. I started smoking on a glass pipe. You see, that was my drug of choice, and it required Brillo. My Brillo would always come up missing and I knew I was not crazy; I knew I had a pipe full of dope to where I could have smoked all day without buying any more, but here I was spending more money and selling things just to get high. I went through this phase as long as I smoked.

Now I was hurt, embarrassed, and ashamed. I'd hurt everyone who ever loved me, and I had no clue what to do. I was getting high to take the pain away, and I was dependent on it. I wanted to quit, but didn't know how. I was arguing with other girls in the house, and stressing because my clothes, earrings, makeup, and shoes kept going missing. To make it worse, Bowlegs didn't care—as a matter of fact he was like a kryptonite playing chess, except the game was being played with my life.

This time on drugs was very difficult and sad…it was the most miserable I have ever been. I started off weighing 145 pounds, and in just 30 days, I had lost 50 pounds. All my money went for drugs. There were days when I had no food to eat. I knew nothing about the streets—I had been out of that world for ten years. All I knew was going to church, reading my Bible, and serving the Lord. Then, when this part of my life came back, I had to learn how to smoke crack. Nobody wanted me to use their pipe—they said I would burn it up. So I had to make sure I had my own glass. As I smoked my crack I grew to understand the fundamentals of it, and that was learning and knowing there was crack thieves hovering around that would follow you and watch you lay your crack down, and still it that was a sign to allow myself to feel crazy.

After a while, I thought I was going crazy, especially when my pipe came looking different than what it was looking like when I set it down. It was like my dope just sucked itself out of the glass, but I didn't get to angry about it. Sure, I was mad, but it was my fault. I chose this life, and I couldn't get mad at the people who were already in this lifestyle. They were surviving, and when I look back on this, I see that God was with me still. He didn't let me put too much in my system. When they thought they were doing something to me, they were hurting themselves all along, and helping me. Thank You, Father—it could have been worse.

I remember sometimes tasting something strange, either in my drink, or when I would go to light up. It burned differently, and had a bad taste. Later on I found out they were trying to drug me with eye drops to put me to sleep. Every time I hit the pipe or took a drink, I felt nauseated and had a bad headache. I asked one of the girls about it and she told me I was being put to sleep so Bowlegs could do his thing. Now I was confused and scared, because this was not the first time I had to undergo this kind of pain. As the days and months went on, I stayed strong, but still sucked on that glass god of mine called a pipe.

Now, on top of everything else going on inside me, I was dealing with not having clothes to wear or makeup to put on. My clothes were missing, so now I was struggling, and I started putting my clothes back in my truck because I was tired of them going missing from the house. Satan had it out for me. I already knew these things were happening to me because I was disobedient to God and not living a godly life.

To top it off, one day Bowlegs came back, and when I went out to my truck, all my clothes were gone. The other females were wearing them. I was finding my clothes in their room. I told him about it, and he said I was crazy, but I knew I wasn't crazy. I knew I needed to change, but it wasn't that easy. My body now craved two things: crack cocaine, and Bowlegs' approval. What was I going to do? I wanted to be with Bowlegs because he was fun to be around. I wanted him to make me feel like the other girls felt. They always had good conversations, but I was always arguing with him, so that made me even more miserable.

There were these guys coming over, buying dope, and I was like the new girl on the block. Nobody ever saw me, and they would always ask, "Who is that?" The other girls must have been in the drug scene for a long time, because when they wanted a girl to spend time and money on, they chose me, and Bowlegs agreed. They would pay him fifty dollars just for fifteen minutes, and I did not do anything with them but sit and talk. When the fifteen minutes was up, they paid him again. He was making good money off me, and I noticed that when I came out of the room he would always be short and the girls would be smoking, and I found out that these females were getting high off the money I made, and also kicking it with my man, but I stayed. I knew no other direction, but through it all, God kept my mind.

I prayed still, and I asked the Lord to give me strength. I didn't know what to do, or how to even think at this moment, and I was hurting inside. My kids were very upset with me, and what did I do? I just kept sucking on that glass god of mine called a pipe, trying to hide the pain of not knowing what to do. I was in a place where other women were wearing my clothes and sleeping with my husband. I loved him, but right now I'm going to tell my testimony, not his, on how the devil taught me how to smoke that crack.

You see, there are different kinds of brillo, and I didn't know it-- one that would burn your dope up, one that would put particles in your throat, and one that carried chemicals that would kill your insides slowly--and trust me, I had a chance to smoke it all. They would play pipe games and switch with me. I called this "the disappearing pipe." It made me feel like the pipe I had in my hand was the same pipe I'd set down, but it wasn't. For months I went through this, killing myself and crying inside because the pain was outrageous, and I had forgotten how bad this kind of life was. I had been with people that loved the Lord for years; I was serving the Lord, and loving it.

I called out to God last time I got this low, and He changed me, just like God told me He would do. I had turned my life around for ten years, but now I was back in the enemy's camp, argu-ing with everybody around me because Bowlegs got everybody thinking I was tripping--and yes, they believed him because they did not want to own up to the truth. They knew what was going on; they were there. At times I thought I was tripping, but I had to pull myself together and remind myself that what was going on was real. They were doing things in my face and I knew what I was seeing, but they told me I was just tripping.

Everybody knew everybody else, and they were close because they helped each other steal from each other. I was the outsider looking into a den of thieves. Sometime I felt like I was crazy, but I know I wasn't. I wouldn't take their bait; I just shined it off. I told myself that one day I was going to get out of there.

I didn't mind bringing up the name of Jesus, and they did too. They would always say, "I'm praying for you," and I would say to myself, "Pray for yourself, because you are going to need it," but I kept smiling, and treated them right no matter what they did to me. I could see that they wanted to change, but they were caught up in their own minds, like I was. They made me feel like I was crazy—I knew I wasn't crazy, but sometimes it really felt like I was.

One day I was in the room smoking dope and my hormones were acting up. Bowlegs had stopped making love to me, and I didn't want anybody else to touch me, so I did myself, not knowing that people were looking at me. They had put holes in the wall, and watched. When I came out of the room, next thing you know I saw people giggling at me. I didn't understand why, and I didn't really care at this point, but eventually I found out. There was a guy who needed a room, and the middle room was empty at this time, so my brother rented him the room, and that's how I found out about the holes in the wall. I knew something was funny about the lock on the door, but I just shook it off; it never would have occurred to me that something like this was going on.

Now I was afraid and paranoid, and Satan was coming at me from every angle. I was tired and ready to quit, but I still had no clue how to do it. Months passed...as a matter of fact, a year passed, and I still hadn't treated anyone differently. I smiled and shared, and even in my distress, I talked about the Lord. One girl came up to me and asked me, "Why don't you hate them?"

I said, "I can't—I'll get out of here someday, and I don't want to have to train myself all over again. I want to keep something inside of me that belongs to God."

Things in my life got worse and worse. You see, I didn't understand witchcraft and how deep and dark it can get, but the Lord showed me how people use it to gain off your life by praying with the devil, and they do get blessed to destroy you by Satan himself, because all along Satan had them fooled into deceitful ways and he is killing them slowly. I used to see these cards--a nine, a seven, an ace of spades--they just would show up around me. At first, I thought nothing of it. It took me a long time to find out that what this is called. It was subliminal messages from my attacker to keep me in bondage. One day a deck of cards was lying in the bathroom and I saw that they had sorcerers and demons and fire coming all out the mouths, and I was asking myself, "What is this?" I read them, and lo and behold, I remembered seeing these attacks on my life. Then the Lord started showing me the demonic sprits that came around me, and they knew when I knew, because they would try to change the game.

As sad as it may seem, my life was a game to Satan, but people did not want to see that. It was real, and they knew it, and they would just say I'm crazy anyway. Anytime I talked about it, they would shine it off, and Satan would bless them. I knew it because things were happing to me so that I was arguing all day, and all my joy was gone. Nobody would answer me when

I asked, "What's with these cards?" All they would say was, "What cards?" and now the crazy was trying to play crazy. I knew what I saw, and that's all that mattered, because now I needed to get wiser with myself. Satan was trying his best to kill me, and I wasn't not blind--now Satan was playing chess with my life, and a lot of the things that were going on around me--for instance, arguing and being frustrated every day—were a part of Satan's tormenting plans to keep me feeling like I needed more drugs.

I stayed angry, and I was a bitter woman. I could not trust anyone, and I practically was feeling some hate toward them, but my heart couldn't hate them because it was not their fault. I would say the blame belonged to the one that was allowing it to happen to me, and that was me. I hated myself. I disliked the ground I walked, on because I changed into a wicked and evil person. At times I would give all my drugs up because I did not like sitting there with someone and knowing that their body was craving too, and then when they would get theirs it was like I didn't matter, and they wouldn't give me anything, so I had to go get it because I have no money for food or for drugs and no one was giving up anything for free.

So I learned how to prostitute, and that was a trade I learned from one of the girls. It was easy money for me, and fast, so I got addicted to that and I would go give my body up. I hated when the men would touch me, but it became my survival kit, because Bowlegs sure was not going to share anything with me... no, not even he would help me. It was like an abandonment feeling going on in me, and I felt left out. It was all I could feel, because I allowed myself to get here and now I didn't know how to get out. As I tell my testimony, I understand what God's Word means when it says you reap what you sow. I did abandon my children; I left them alone to fend for themselves. I walked away into my own lust and I'd like to say I'm sorry, to all my kids. Let me go on, and I pray that whoever reads my testimony that it helps you find your glory in God, and not in people or in the things that we think are happiness.

Now my truck was gone and my clothes were in the house. I was keeping my clothes in boxes, the little that I had, and now I was feeling stupid—I was asking myself, "Is this really going on, or am I tripping?" One minute I would see a lot of my clothes, and the next minute I would see a small amount. At first I thought I was tripping, but one of the girls owned up to it and said, "You're right; it does look life half of your clothes is gone."

I laughed at the situation and said, "If they've got that much energy to keep doing this, then good luck!" and I didn't let it bother me anymore, because I saw that it was to keep me upset to where I couldn't think, try to drive me crazy, and it seemed like once I got through one problem, here came another one. Now I was having a problem with my soap and lotion—the problem had always been there, but I just didn't notice until all this showed up. When I bought my soap, it had lather, so when I left it in the bathroom and came back, I could tell it was different. It took me a long time to figure this out, because I didn't think stuff like this existed—they were taking my soap and mixing it up with chemicals. You see, everybody would always tell me that my legs were beautiful. I guess the enemy hated that, and used it to stop me from smiling, when he wanted me to be killing myself, which I was doing slowly. My legs were starting to look like fish scales, and when I put my lotion on it just dried out my pores. Now I wouldn't wear anything that showed my legs. I don't know what they put in that lotion, but my skin was turning dark like dirt, and I guess when I took a shower I wasn't washing anything off anyway; I was just putting more dirt and who knows what else inside me. My soap had no suds and my lotion had no mellow, and my life was sadder than sad...but still God kept me.

One day, I cut my hair real short so I could put my extensions in, but I had to use glue to put the hair on. On this particular day, I was doing my hair, and I noticed later that I got sores on my scalp and my head was burning up. And guess what? Someone put perm solution inside my glue. When I smelled my bottle, it was not right. I cried and I argued, but same result came right back to me—they said I was crazy and tripping, and you know what? The devil was so good at using people--he knew just the right ones to pick out...the ones who can't stand you or who are just plain old jealousies of you. People will try to make you feel like you're crazy, but don't let anybody make you feel like what's going on around you isn't real. It's real, Satan is real, and if you're called by God, Satan knows it--but do you know? Well, look at yourself and ask that again. Look at where you're standing. Are you standing in the enemy's camp right now? Are you getting all beat up like me?

I cried every day. I allowed myself to suffer in a way that smothered me, to where I felt there was no way to escape, but I still stayed the same. I lived under the attack of Satan for two and a half years, not knowing where my strength was. It got so bad that living in my brother's house was a nightmare on Drummond Street. Now the devil wasn't hiding the women; he was placing them in my face, and they were boldly wearing my clothes. It had now been a year and some months, and it seemed like the females were walking in through the walls, but I knew better now. Bowlegs had his own room, and I slept on the couch. We were totally not together at this time. It did not matter to me anymore because now I was tired and frustrated and really wanted to change, so I cried to God to help me and show me what to do, but seemed like my problem got worse.

We had another roommate living in the house. He had his room, and he would go along with Bowlegs and play the game and hide the girls in one room, and they would walk into his when he thought I wasn't paying attention. I knew that these females were in his room. I would hear them talking, but I overlooked it. He did not want me, even though I wanted him. It seemed like the more I craved for him, the worse it got--even my craving for him was something strange, because he was not hiding those women anymore. They walked right in the room with him, as if I was not standing there. Here I was, playing the game too—I called it the survival kit. I played into the satanic cat and mouse game because I felt that Bowlegs did not want me in his life anyway, so I got with my boys and I told my sons and my nephew what was going on. They saw it, because Bowlegs didn't hide anything, but he got away with it, and Satan did bless him.

I told them that I had no other place to go and this was my brother's house and I had to do something just to eat and supply my drug habit. But I needed to change the game of respect and have some men friends. They wanted to kick it with me anyway and pay, me so why not? Bowlegs was doing it, and I told them because Bowlegs would get mad when the tables turned and argue with me. He didn't want me, but he didn't want anybody else to have me, and they would stop him from getting in my face. But every time we would get together and get into each other for some reason, someone would knock on the door. It was as if we were not supposed to connect. We both got tired of that, and it took a lot out of him, because now he didn't care to be with me, and now I had to enjoy him and his so-called friends in the room with him, and when I would say something these females would actually have the nerve to say, "This is my friend and I'm not going to stop coming to see him." Deep down inside I wanted to let those females have it, but it would always end with him saying something smart to me and protecting them, and I just left it alone because all I could see was me walking away from this someday and I wasn't going to allow my self-worth to be destroyed for anybody.

I dressed as if I was not a user, so now my clothes were disappearing big time. I had told myself that I might be on the crack pipe, but I wasn't going to look like a smoker. So when they threw out the trash, I went digging in that trash for clothes, because I told myself there wasn't any point in saving up money to buy clothes when they would just disappear anyway. I found some good clothes, and some time these clothes were brand-new--but lo and behold, they walked away, and in all this I found a new drug to smoke on and I used it just to keep me awake so I would not go to sleep. This drug was called crystal meth and I mixed it together with crack cocaine, and I also was taking pills and smoking weed and drinking at the same time just to survive. I smoked four packs a cigarettes of any kind for two and a half years, not knowing regular from unregular.

You see, I was troubled in spirit, and my soul was vexed from the decisions I had made in my life, and all this troubled me because I loved someone too much. I made him my god and was looking for him to deliver me by just loving and respecting me. I was trying to do everything a woman is supposed to do for her man, just to get his approval. I tried hard to love him, and I just stayed in a bad situation. Since I was his wife, I felt I had the right to say whatever the heck I wanted to say to any of those females, and all I wanted was respect—for them not to call him baby or try to show how much fun they had with him. In other words, I didn't want them to brag to me about it, because that was a problem.

I was already hurting inside because he did not want me, and I had to learn to accept that. I told myself I had to change, because what I was going through right now, no human should have to feel. This kind of a pain will drive the insane crazier, so I just told myself over and over that one day I would walk away from this somehow--something had to change in me. And on New Year's Day, that was when everything I had gone through really hit me. I knew it was time to walk away before I ended up in prison or someone ended up dead, and I told myself this would not be the case. The love of my life, the one I put before everything including my own happiness, somebody that I allowed to run over me and do terrible things to me...I decided that I would not live another day with this kind of person, where the wind was blowing only one way, and it wasn't my way.

I told myself, "Enough is enough" when 2012 came and he shared his life with another woman in New Year's Eve. All New Year's Day, I swallowed my pain and held my tongue. I had nothing to eat and no dope to smoke. I was hurting and suffering and all I could do was sing to myself and say I was going to get out. At that moment, I said to myself, "This man is not worth my life or my time." Now that I look back, God saved me, but the devil still had a hold on my life with strongholds, and that was loving Bowlegs too much. The Bible is right when it says the devil comes back seven times worse with more demons. He did, and some evil ones came with him. I thought about my situation and I said to myself, I will talk with my kids, my mother, and my sisters. I told my nephew, "I got to go--I got to get out before I end up somewhere I don't want to be."

So here I am today. I called up the same pastor that told me I had to leave, and he agreed to help me. He and my sister got together and paid for my plane ticket, and my niece got all the arrangements together, and I had a week to leave. I told myself that Saturday if I was to live, that would be my last day of juggling with the devil--and I made it, so when Sunday came I called my mother and told her to come get me. Mama said, "I'm not dressed yet."

I said, "Mama, please, come on," and she said she was on her way. I had my bags packed, and I was ready to go. I was serious. The Lord said to call on Him, and I did. I spent the day with my mother and kids, and on Monday morning my son and his wife took me to LA and I caught my plane and here I am in Chicago, Illinois, writing my story.

I lived in Chicago for six months, going to church, building character, and getting growth. I got baptized in Chicago and then started going to one of the churches out there and got taught the Word, and I was ready. They prayed for me and gave me strength. My new family gave me hope to live again, and I was ready to go back to Fresno because I was going through so much up in Chicago. It was time to go, so I came home back to Fresno, California and moved in with my daughters. I was doing well, going to church, reading my Bible, being a part of the sisterhood, and I was ready to serve the Lord. A month passed, and I was still clean. I started my divorce papers, feeling good about where I was going. I had a dream now—I wanted to help women to understand their self-worth.

But did I stop? No. Did I go back? Yes. On December 9th, I got with Bowlegs, and it was a rap. I can't blame him, only myself, because I let go, and I hurt a lot of people. Once again, I fell. Did it bother me? Yes, it suffocated me. Had anything changed since I left? No—everything was the same. It was the same situation, and I stayed locked up in that for five months. I got tired of it and I called a few places to try to get into a drug rehab program, because I had lost all trust with my family, and I didn't blame them. I had to regain my family's trust.

One of the drug rehab centers said I could come on a Tuesday for an interview, but it was already Tuesday, and I missed the appointment they had for that day. I wanted this change right now—tomorrow might be too late. I called another place, and he said to call back in fifteen minutes. I did, and he told me to call back in five minutes. I did, and when I called, he forgot who I was. He asked me what I needed. I told him I needed an inpatient program. He started telling me about the program, and I was excited, because it was what I needed. Then he told me what it cost. He said I needed $4000 for six months, or $1000 for 30 days. I was on drugs. I didn't have that kind of money, so I said, "Sorry, wrong program." There was another program I could have gone to, but I had sold drugs to the staff and smoked with them, and I wasn't going to be part of that lie—I might as well stay at my brother's house, because there were more drugs in that program than there were on the street. I was trying to get off, not pick up a new habit.

The Holy Spirit had me call my mother. I did, and she allowed me to live with her, and the grace of God allowed me to do this again. Today I share with you: Don't get out for someone else. Do it for yourself. Don't get out for your mama, sister, brother, and auntie, uncle, kids, or grandkids— get out because you really want it. Get out because you're tired of serving in Satan's kingdom, doing nothing and only destroying yourself. Tell yourself, like I did that day: "Father, I can't do this alone. My drug is not the drug itself; it's the man." I had to realize that he was my high—as long as I had him, that was all I wanted, and God gave me a way of escape by letting me see that when I was delivered from the drugs, I was also delivered from Bowlegs, and He also delivered me from the streets. But I never asked Him to deliver me from the love I had for Bowlegs, but my love was not a healthy love, and I needed a healthy love for him, and that love is to help bring him out from under the tormenting spirits that also control him. Today I'm blessed; I'm clean from everything, and it is only God Himself who keeps me. I place His Word in my heart now, and I must leave it there in order to do kingdom work that keeps me strong. Greater is He that is in me than he that is in the world.

Now I'm grounded again in a church home that loves me, and a family that fears God. I want to tell the world that the devil is a liar. We are stronger than we think we are--we can get out. When it seems dark, there is light at the end of that tunnel. Just believe that God never leaves you nor forsakes you (Hebrews 13:5). I walked away; I've been clean and going to church. I've repented of my sins and have asked God for forgiveness, and He has forgiven me, and I have forgiven myself. Not only that--I told everybody that was out there on them drugs that I hurt before I even left to forgive me so I can really receive the anointing in my life, because I have things to do for God. I have visions that I had before I stepped out there in the world, but now I have greater visions than those, and with the Lord's help I want to give God's glory back by sharing my testimony with lost sheep of God's pasture, building buildings that will offer genuine love for my sisters and brothers who are lost out in the world and tangled up in Satan's headquarters, and thinking that they can't make it. I want to open up a home that God has shown me that will give them hope in knowing that someone does care about their future, believing that they can change. I would like to give back what I have learned and what I have seen, and what it takes for one to be strong--and that is Jesus Christ. He is the only way. Everyone that reads my book, I pray that you will be inspired to understand that we must not we place anything or anybody before God. Our are happiness comes from God; our peace comes from God; our joy comes from God--and in all that we find either the peace that passes all understanding, or we find the peace that only God can give. May God bless you.

# I KNEW ONE DAY

I KNEW ONE day I was going to get out. I believed in myself that I was going to make it through, and guess what? I did. I made up my mind a long time ago. I would always say, "Soon," or "In a little while." I would cry to God and say, "Please now, Lord--I'm tired; no more!" Sometime I would be in a tired three-day run. Then I really got tired, but I had to make sure that it wasn't the tired that came from being up too long. I examined myself really thoroughly by asking myself, "Am I sure I am really ready to stop?" I looked at myself and all that was around me, and said, "This isn't me—I have tasted the remnant of the good of God, and this remnant of Satan is wearing me down, destroying me, giving me no hope, no joy, and much sadness." I had been chasing after the wind. A wind chaser is someone just blowing around with no direction in their life, and that's what I was: a wind chaser, with no direction, lost in the foulness of Satan's lies. I looked at the good that was in me and I said, "I'm better than this," and I walked away more than once, but I knew one day it would be for real. Look, this is for real, and I'm going ahead strong, with no shame about my past, but I am going to tell the world how God answered my cry--and not only that; I will show how in my life He gave me strength while I obeyed his commands, because without a covering of obedience toward God, there is no life; there is only death, because I will obey until God says, "Well done, good and faithful servant."

I pray to be a light to the lost, and an example to those who feel that all is lost. No, it isn't, but only in obedience to God will you be saved, and it starts with accepting God go be your personal savior, to help you maintain your dignity. That's called self-control. As you are asking God for forgiveness, you have to forgive yourself, and then accept the lifestyle that God will offer you, and that is in obedience to Him and Him only. All else will follow.

Amen, amen.

# WE GAVE UP; WE GAVE IN

WE GAVE UP; we gave in; we stopped. Why did we stop? What did we stop for? What did we see? What did we want? Why did we agree upon the lie that faced us, a lie that we knew was not real, a lie that we should have understood? We read the Word, we heard the preacher; we even heard it in a song. So what made us so weak, especially when we just knew God was all we wanted to serve? What happened? Did we get bored? Did we get helpless? Did we get forgetful? Whatever it was, we changed the plan of God's hand. We made it harder for ourselves; we became stiff-necked people who allowed the flesh to back us up, and slow us down, and take us into bondage that choked the Word away.

But God says that His Word will never leave us. We might get all tangled and twisted inside and get off track like I did, because this was me in this world; I got where I did not want to listen to and do the will no more, because it seemed boring and hard at the time, and I let Satan feed on that, and I got all messed up and stayed in the wilderness for a very long time, never understanding until I said to myself, "I'm tired," and I cried every day to the Lord, "Help me--I can't take it anymore--this wilderness has no feeling and no future." Every day it was the same old page— plenty of sadness, trying to make something out of nothing, and feeling empty, void of my own illusion that never leaves…we just put it to the side, and get hard-headed, to where we don't want to listen to the spirit of God because our flesh runs the program. So today I say, God is running this program, Satan, not you. God has heard my cry.

Amen, amen.

# TODAY I HAD

TODAY I HAD to put my body and mind under my control, and let myself know that I was not going to just lie there in that bed defeated, because that is not what I came to Chicago to do.

I didn't come here to let my body sleep, as if it's just lost, and out of control. So I had to say to this body of mine, "Get up— and I mean *get up*!"

I had to talk to this body as I am talking to you right now. I had to tell this flesh, "Get up, and get in order, because laziness is not of God, and cleanliness is next to Him. Get up," I said to my body, mind, and soul. "Get up!"

And you know what was funny? 12:00 p.m. rolled around. I got up, looked at the clock, and went back to sleep. Next thing you know, I was looking at 1:00 p.m. on the dot, just the same as I did at 12:00 p.m.

But this time, I said, "No more!" I got up, cleaned my room, and while I took a shower, I cleaned the bathroom. Let me remind you that I needed the gospel station to help with the anointing; that was needed to flow throughout the whole house…and here I am today to say: "We must speak to the mountain, which was my flesh. I had to tell it what it must do."

We must put the flesh under subject and under the authority of God, into what we need it to do for our lives to have completeness. And I thank God that I got up, because here I am today to tell it all—to tell of the victory of Jesus Christ, who came and gave me the authority to tell this flesh, "Get up, and get with the program." The program is to tell the testimony of how God redeemed me, through His Son, so I can talk to the mountain and tell the mountain to get in order. So talk to your mountain, and tell it you are more than a conqueror in Jesus Christ. (Romans 8:37)

Amen, and amen.

# BELIEVERS ARE ROOTED

IN EVERYTHING, BELIEVERS are rooted first and foremost in Him, alive in Him, hidden in Him, clothed in Him, and complete in His love, with His peace ruling their hearts. We must make Christ equipped in every area of our life. We must learn the trademark that holds the depth within us. We are called the chosen. He said in His Word, in Peter 2:9, "But ye are a chosen generation, a particular people, that ye should show forth the praises of Him who hath called you out of darkness into His marvelous light."

Because believers are rooted in Him, it is utterly inconsistent for them to live life without Him, or without being complete in Him. I have learned that I must breathe in the aroma of God's love, and eat the food in which is His Word. And when I say eat, I mean it has to be more than breakfast, lunch, and dinner, because I have seen the enemy at hand, because I was watching everybody else go to church, and sing and dance in the choir. I was watching people shouting and praising. I was looking at the preacher and the deacon and the ushers, and things that were being done that were contrary to the will of God; they were still partying and doing unholy things. That's not following the will of God; that's playing church.

So you are trying to really live—and I mean really trying to do it. What happens? You get choked by the enemy himself because now you're lonely, confused, upset, and disillusioned about the whole aspect of God. Today I learned a valuable lesson. I learned to read the Word for myself, and move on. I was looking at people, and instead I needed to look at the One who made me, because people aren't perfect—they are only doing what they have seen others do. They feel like its okay, but it's not okay. Satan has wrapped our minds into the eyes of seeing instead of the eyes that understand the Word. I say to you today, as well as to myself, "Let's be Christ-like." As the Bible says in James 1:22, "Be ye doers of the Word and not hearers, only deceiving your own selves." Therefore, we can help to save the next generation.

Amen, and amen.

# TODAY

LORD, I THANK you today. I'm not mingled in mess and all distressed, feeling like something with no rest, or wiggled in wine, in messed-up wine that has the sour of a porcupine. I'm not worried about the world around me or the people I see, because the gift You've given me has sustained me to be the victor and not the victim to the pain I've seen or the stain that was given me. I'm grateful today I've got peace of mind; You have given me a love that keeps my mind sustained with a future that has something. Lord, You brought me out; You made me be somebody and not the nobody that they tried to make me. You made me a part of you, and I'm so happy right now today I truly can shout hallelujah. They did not kill me nor take my mind; I can write and tell my story how the enemy tried to triumph over my life--but I won the battle of disillusion, and I thank You, Lord.

Amen, and amen.

# PEOPLE SORRY

HAVE YOU EVER been around people who love to give orders, but can't take orders themselves? I call them people sorry--selfish people who want nothing but to run your life by living their life in you, because they cannot and will not live the real life that is in them, but want to direct your life into what they feel it should look and feel like for their own selfish gain. Do you know people like this? This is not you, is it? In 1 Corinthians 3:18, it says, "Let no man deceive himself. If any man among you seemeth to be wise in this world, let him become a fool that he may be wise, for the wisdom of this world is foolishness with god. For it is written, He teaches the wise in his own craftiness. And again, the Lord knoweth the thoughts of the wise that they are in vain. Therefore let no man glory in men, for all things are yours."

The Word has corrected me today, because I was lost in a world that controlled and led me. I let people think for me, tell me when and how far to jump, and where to go. Today I read my Bible, and now the Lord is leading me, and when I get confused, I fall on my knees and call to the Lord and get still somewhere until He answers. Sometimes it feels like He's not answering fast enough for me, but He has been on time all the time. So I leave you with this: If you are in a predicament of this manner, where you're either the controller or the controlled, fall on your knees and pray and ask God to build character in you to what He has made you to be, and not what people sorry want you to be. Find your true identity that lies inside of you. God gave each of us one, you see. Today I have taken control over me, and now God controls me. And I thank Him for His Son, Jesus. That gave me my identity.

Amen, and amen.

# DON'T WANT

WHEN I SAY I don't want to do something, I am really meaning that I don't want to do nothing. Because I don't feel like doing some things sometimes, and I have my reasons; I might be stubborn in a lot of ways, but I have come a long way to get here. I have been through the going and the coming of moving too fast, especially when it was not God talking to me, and I have wasted a lot of my energy on things that were not of god, doing things that made no sense, because they got me nowhere but right back in the same boat—no growth, no plan, just doing nothing. Today I'm looking for the best, and that's the Word, so I can renew my mind to be able to get the hope, joy, peace, and love that will keep me, and I will be able to be energized to do the things that I'm really called to do, and I will know that it will go forth because it will be the will of God and not just of doing, because I can do a lot of things that won't mean anything. Today I choose to please God. I choose not movement, but to stand still and know that I hear His voice, because the Holy Spirit that lives in me will let me know the Word.

Amen, and amen.

# FINDING TIME SPENT

FINDING TIME SPENT with me has been the best time. Of my life. I remember when I could not smell, I couldn't see, I couldn't hear or feel my own self-worth. I had held on to a life in such a way that I couldn't understand that Why was my first name, and Jones was my last name...because I didn't know that "jones" was another name for the addiction I held on to, making something out of nothing, which was the drugs I had used for a very long time. I spent many days doing things that I regret, so that Why became my first name. I would always say, "Why did I do that?" I would beat myself up in a way that I couldn't think. I was in love with what I thought was good for me. I believed that if I could show my self-worth, then I would be loved back, but I found out that no person or thing can love me if it can't love itself first. So I started spending time with me, getting to know myself and satisfy myself, and when I did that, then I was able to hear the Holy Spirit speak to me and tell me that God loves me, and He is here with me. That's when my change came--spending time with me, loving me first, and now I'm seeking God and He is loving me. That's what I should have been doing all that time, if only I would have known better. So here I am to say to you: place yourself above all else but God. In God's Word, Proverbs 3:6, it says, "In all thy ways acknowledge Him, and He shall direct your paths." Today I am a living example of that. Believe in yourself first that you are loved, and you will never have to place "why" over and over in your life. Today my first name is Diane, and my last name is Hall--the name that God gave me to be delivered and loved by Him and in Him.

SPEND TIME WITH yourself first and get to know who you are...

AND ALL ELSE WILL FOLLOW.

Amen, and amen.

# FIRST AND FOREMOST

FIRST AND FOREMOST, Lord, I want to say thank You for waking me up this morning, and getting me started on my way. You didn't have to do it, but you did. Glory and honor are yours; and mercy and grace are mine. Thank You. You gave me a mind to think, a mind to feel my own thoughts. You gave me eyes to see my own way. You gave me a mouth to talk, to say my own words. You gave me feet to walk in my own direction. You gave me ears to hear my own essence. You gave me hands to hold on to my own change. You gave me a heart that beats, and it tells me and shows me my own desire. You gave me a love so sweet that only Jesus could cover it, so that I can love all my brothers and sisters. And these are the stones that make a home that will follow me and make me strong—stronger than I've ever been. He has made me strong, and He shall make you strong as well, so believe in the tools of God's Word.

"But thanks be to God which gives us the victory through our Lord Jesus Christ. (1 Corinthians 15:57)

Amen, and amen.

# MAKING AWAY

YOU KNOW WHAT, Lord? I thank you. People can't hurt me anymore; all they can do for me is make me strong. And when I say strong, I mean stronger. Yes, I have been helped; yes, I have been saved; and yes, the reward that I have been given shall be great in return, and this is to the giver and the taker, because without you I would not have made it this far into the greater vision that God has given me. Today I will respect them both, because both of them have given me strength to see what lies ahead in my life. When the taker was taking things from me, he did not know that he was building me up for the Kingdom of God, because he showed me things that I do not want to do to someone else. To hurt someone else for selfish gain is not of God. To make someone feel low and unworthy is not of God. To cause suffering and hurt to someone has shown me that the pain is real, and that has shown me the pain that Jesus went through to get me here today. It was rough and hard, and it was a long, hard, and lonely journey, because people can't see or feel the hurt they place on someone, unless they have been through it.

I say to the giver: Thank you for your encouraging words. Thank you for being there for me when I couldn't see. When the taker was stealing my soul, you were there to give me hope. You allowed God to breathe into you and give me life. We need more givers of love like you. I don't care where a person stands in life; if we just give back, God will be able to allow that person to feel and see himself better. Because sometimes all a person needs is an ear to hear, so they can know that the scriptures are real—especially Isaiah 54:17, which says, "No weapon that is formed against thee shall prosper, and every tongue that shall rise against thee in judgment, thou shalt condemn. This is the heritage of the servants of the Lord, and their righteousness is of me, says the Lord.

Amen, and amen.

# ONE THING

ONE THING I am learning, and I do know for a fact, is that I must stay prayed up. I must learn to be serious about the kingdom of God; I must be serious about God's business; I must know and I must believe in myself and know what I truly want, heaven are hell; I must have a mindset knowing that this is not a game of life, with a board that you put back in the closet when you're done. I must learn to believe in myself with a sincere heart, mind, body, and soul. It's going to take all three to get lined up for the body to understand the way of a Christian livelihood, because we take a lot of things for granted in this world, thinking that we are In the right perspective of God, and we blind ourselves, not knowing that the way of God is knowing Him.

And how do we get to know Him? By reading His Word. That helps with the mind; it gives you structure in knowing what to do. It's the road map to understanding, because without understanding, how can you know what to do or even how to act in this world? The word teaches the mind so the body can learn how to act; it puts it into subjection to the Word of God and allows your soul to identify the craving that is within you, so put all three of these together and you will be able to live out your vision…and in that you will be able to really know if you choose heaven or hell. I have come to a point in my life that living for God has been the best--He has made all things possible (1 John 4:4). Greater is He that is in me, thin he that is in the world, and who should be in me? God the Father, God the Son, and God the Holy Spirit—three in one.

Spiritual foundation is

1. Read the Word

2. Pray ask God for direction

3. Listen to gospel music that cures the soul

4. Go to church to find believers

5. Stay positive

And in all that you will survive.

Amen, and amen.

# TODAY

TODAY I WILL say it's another day of strength, another day of goodness. Even though its morning and I have not reached my evening or my night, I still claim another day of goodness and strength. I do know without a doubt that when joy comes, also sadness tries to creep in, but I know the Word tells me to focus and keep my mind on God's Word, and it will refrain anything that will try to hinder the goodness of God, because God is good. And He is good enough for me. There is a song that goes:

I know God is a good God

Yes He is

I know God is a good God

Yes He is

I say God is a loving God

Yes He is

And that song gives me the power to believe and know that that's all I need, so be blessed. And know that God is a good God for me and for you.

Amen, and amen.

# WATCH AND PRAY

AS LONG AS you're out there in the world, Satan cares when you want to serve God. So what are you going to do? Satan has a plot and a plan to change the way you think. He likes to put things in your way and in your mind so you can keep your mind off God. What are you going to do? In the world, things keep going, and the world looks good... it looks like a big bright light of fun, but there is nothing but darkness that flows in the four corners of the world. The bible says (Romans 12:2) be in the world, but not of the world.

Amen, and amen.

# STAND FOR GOD

DANIEL STOOD FOR God and did not give up. He was a strong Christian. Daniel had the ability to be strong and Satan tried to strip him of it, because he did not want Daniel to be strong for God or even for himself. That's how Satan plays on us, because he knows that we belong to God, so he uses tactics on us, and one is called fear, to make us believe that God has not chosen us to be kids of the kingdom. But God will open up your mind and eyes, so you can see the devil for who he is. But we need to train ourselves by disciplining our body and mind to understand how to live for God. We must walk with Him so he can show us the things to come--you will have to walk with God; you will have to talk to God, on a daily basis. Satan wants people to be godless--he wants people to desire him, and he is the things that unqualified us from God, and those are the things of this world. I was into those things: drugs, money, sex, lying, stealing, and alcohol...you name it. If it didn't deal with God, I desired it.

I realized one day that I have a calling on my life, and it is no accident that I am here in this world today. I was born to serve God and God alone. Satan messed me up, and I allowed him to. I got this scripture--I have repeated it more than once in these pages, but this is what I live on today. It is 1 John 4:4, "Greater is He that is in me than he that is in the world." I have been kept by His new mercies that He gives to me each and every day, and I love myself today. So I say to you my brother, my sister--look around you. If it's not looking like God, get away from it. It's only there to keep you from the will of God, so teach yourself how to control the better part of you, and only you. Know what that is. I did, and look at me—I'm writing, and telling my story.

Amen, and amen.

# SOMETIMES

I KNOW SOMETIMES when you open up your eyes, it seems like the problem is still there—like Satan is just sitting up waiting for your eyes to open, just to see what you're going to do...and he is. But thank God for being God, because he is also waiting to remind you of the scriptures. "The Lord is my light and my salvation, whom shall I fear? The Lord is the strength of my life, of whom shall I be afraid? When the wicked, even mine enemies and my foes came upon me to eat up my flesh, they stumbled and fell. Though a host should encamp against me, my heart shall not fear, though war shall rise against me. In this will I be confident, for in the time of trouble He shall hide me in His pavilion. In the secret of His tabernacle shall He hide me. He shall set me up upon a rock, and now shall mine head be lifted up above my enemies round about me: therefore will I offer in His tabernacle sacrifices of joy: I will sing praises unto the Lord. And in that, Satan can wait as long as he wants, because one thing have I desired of the Lord, that I will seek after; that I may dwell in the house of the Lord all the days of my life, to behold the beauty of the Lord and to enquire in His temple." (Psalms 27 1-2-3-5-6-4)

Amen, and amen.

# BURDEN BEARER

EVERYBODY HAS A service, because everybody has a burden in this world. Young and old are placed in different places for the ministry by the calling of God. The service of ministry is playing, listening, talking, or hugging…taking the time out to offer yourself and your time in love. This is called the ministry of giving. But first we must learn how to be strong in God alone, in order to help lift burdens through the name of Jesus Christ, so we can help other people. That could be our brother or sister, nephew, niece, mother, grandmother, grandfather, father, cousin, uncle, aunt, son, daughter, friend or enemy. We must learn to be good listeners for the body of Christ. Sometimes people just want you to listen, or give them a hug, or they just need a word of encouragement. A soft word spoken heals the soul. We must know the Word of God in order to help fight the enemy that brings these burdens.

People need encouragement just to get through the day. A smile can do it, and don't forget sometimes to say, "I love you, and God is with you." Give them a scripture. We are in God, and it will come from God. Tell them, "God bless you." It is something that will make you feel good. Give it to the burden carrier, because burdens are heavy to carry. Even though we should know who to place our burdens on, sometimes we have to be reminded. That's why, if we all give to each other the same, then it will become like an epidemic with power for the kingdom of God.

MATTHEW 11:28-30

"Come unto me all ye that labor and are heavy laden, and I will give you rest. Take my yoke upon you, and learn of me, for I am meek and lowly in heart: and ye shall find rest unto your souls, for my yoke is easy, and my burden is light."

So be a shield for the burden bearer as well as for yourself, and your burden shall be lifted.

Amen, and amen.

# TEARS OF JOY

TEARS OF JOY are the best to have, because they give you strength, just to know that you have conquered, and the place where you are. The moment when tears of joy fall is the greatest moment, because whatever troubled you, or whatever you went through—guess what? You made it through. I made it through some difficult days that hung around on my plate, days when sometimes I did not even want to wake up, because I knew what lay in front of me: a day without hope. Sometimes it was hard even to breathe, because when I looked around at my situation, it was like every day was the same. I didn't know what time it was or what day it was...I was just in another day of pain.

But today my tears are tears of joy—tears that have sustained me with the victory of knowing my tomorrow is blessed and kept by the Father of all, who sent His only begotten Son, Jesus Christ, to free me from the dark cloud that tried to choke me and make me hold on to the real tears. Today my tears are what make me stronger, knowing that the tears of sorrow I held on to have turned into good, as they were meant to do. Now I can say to myself, "That storm is over." Now I don't have to look back at that storm anymore, or cry into it. God has delivered me, and He will do the same for you, but you have to want to be delivered. I wanted to be delivered, and I asked God to help me, and He came to my rescue. Now my tears have turned from sadness to joy.

Amen, and amen.

# THIS IS MY LIFE

THIS IS MY life today, and I wouldn't trade it for a million dollars. I wouldn't trade it for diamonds, or gold, or rubies, or sapphires, because it's a life that's perfect for me—a life with no shame, a life that gives hope, a life with feelings, a life that shares no pain but the pain of knowing what Jesus had to carry for me to get here today. It was the crucifixion and the shedding of His blood that gave me my today. The Father loved me enough to say, "Diane, here is My Son—I give Him to you, so you can have life more abundantly." And I thank God, because I had some very imperfect days going on in my life, but as soon as I said yes to God, He said yes to me. I get up every day now and I don't have to look over my shoulder or worry about my next moment. I get up and grab my Word that is hidden inside me, and it gives me no thought of guilt of where I have been or the trouble I shared. I live with peace of mind, knowing that my help cometh from the Lord. If only I keep my lifestyle in line with His Word, I can live like this until the Lord says it's time to come home. Today I want to be an example, a light to let you know there is life in living in God. There is stability and strength, but God gives us a choice to choose our way. You have to desire change; you have to want it for yourself. Nobody but you can give it to yourself—and how do you do that? You do it like I did. I fell on my knees and cried out, "Lord, help me—I can't do this by myself any-more. I'm tired of looking over my shoulder, wondering what will happen next. I want to live in peace now. I need my family to have a safety net while I'm still alive…to have something to look for besides hate and cruelty going on around them." I remembered a preacher saying, "Ask for forgiveness, and God will sup with you." That means that if I ask for help, God will come and be with me, because He will hear my cry for change.

That's what I did—I took one step and He took two, and ever since, He has been taking some mighty big steps in my life, one after another. But I am sincere in my change, and about living a different life, so no…I will not give this life of Christ up for anything. There is nothing else that can or will give me what I have now: the peace that passes all understanding. Like my sister said, I don't understand it either, but it's the best. Try it!

Amen, and amen.

# (1 Chronicles 7:14)

"IF MY PEOPLE which are called by my name would humble themselves, and pray and seek my face, and turn from their wicked ways; then will I hear from Heaven, and will forgive their sin, and will heal their land."

I have used this scripture for my life, and it has given me the change that I would not give up.

Amen, and amen.

# LIFE

WHAT IS LIFE without answers to questions to direct a path that holds a person's ability to stand and be strong, and understand the way to life? Life has an ability to be destroyed or to be alive. It's up to the individual to live the path that he must go. No one can tell anyone what to do or not do—it's up to the individual, because he holds the key to his own control. Even God gives that freely to understand His own way. God gives us a choice to live our own life. Life will have ups and downs; it gives smiles and it gives frowns. But we must stay strong through it all. We must hold our head up, and not look down.

(Psalms 117)

"Praise the Lord, all ye nations! Praise Him all, all you people of the world. His mercy toward us is powerful. The Lord's faithfulness endures forever."

Amen, and amen.

# I CLAIM

I CLAIM SALVATION in my life, I claim God's authority in my life, I claim victory in my life, I claim morals in my life, I claim holiness over my life, I claim prayers over my life, I claim goodness over my life, I claim safety over my life, I claim vision over my life, I claim thankfulness over my life, I claim functions over my life, I claim joy over my life, I claim peace over my life, I claim unity over my life, I claim sound doctrine over my life, I claim completeness over my life, I claim wholeness over my life, I claim the Holy Spirit over my life, I claim Jesus over my life. And in all this being claimed over my life, I know that God will do a perfect work in me, because in all this, I have power.

God arms me with strength and makes my way perfect (Psalms 18:32) especially if I claim all this in my life.

Amen, and amen.

# BUILD YOURSELF UP

I MUST BUILD my own strength. If I want Jesus to be a part of my life, then I must do what it takes for me to get there, because Sunday is gone and Thursday is too long, and here I am at Tuesday, and I am afraid to be empty because Satan himself kicks back on Monday, Tuesday, and Wednesday, just waiting to get me out of and up from under the will of God, because he realizes that Thursday and Sunday are all I see. But I've come to a conclusion in my life—that I need to be filled at all points and times in this life of mine. I must continue in the faith and believe in myself, not worrying about the next day trying to get in the building. God has made a way for me. I can get it on the internet; I can get it on the TV or the radio, and I can read the Word for myself and ask God to help me understand. I have found that I must learn every day, every waking hour of my life, to see, hear, touch, smell, and move in God's anointing, because Satan is on his job to frustrate the Word right out of me with discouraging appointments. So I tell you today, don't wait for Sunday or Thursday night. Get yours seven days a week, twenty-four hours a day, because the weapons of this warfare are not carnal. We do not deal with flesh and blood; we deal with principalities that sit in dark places. Scripture tells us this— read Ephesians 6:11-12. We must put on the full armor of God, that we may be able to stand against the wiles of the devil. Just read Ephesians Chapter 6 and learn of this warfare.

Amen, and amen.

# UNLESS

UNLESS A MAN builds his house, his house won't stand. Unless a man stands on the Word of God, he cannot build. Unless you believe, you cannot receive. Unless you hold out, you cannot reach out. Unless you have been through, you cannot see through. Unless you know rain, you can't see pain. Unless you are willing, you have no feelings. Unless you get strong, you will stay weak. Unless you try, you will not buy. Unless you give in to God's way and only His way, you will not see the victory. It's God's way, or the highway to destruction. Unless this is all you want, this is all you will receive, and unless you want change, you will remain the same. I believe I've said more than enough.

Amen, and amen.

# I KNOW

TODAY I HAVE accepted and know that the pain I have had inside of me for so long, the sadness and emptiness I have carried all these years, kept deep down, not wanting to believe the truth—now I know it's time, truly time to live my life, and go get what will make all this go away. But first, I must start with a plan, I must put something together, so I think I'll start here.

1. Have I accepted it? Yes.

2. Am I willing? Yes.

3. Is it okay? Yes.

4. Am I ready to let it all go? Yes.

5. Am I ready to forgive and forget? Yes.

6. Am I ready to move on? Yes.

7. Okay, now I can start!

8. But wait—I have to divorce Satan. Am I ready? Yes.

9. Now this, I see, means being free.

10. Now let me go on. Thank You, Lord, because without the Holy Spirit in me, I would not have known the steps.

Amen, and amen

# LOVING ME

LOVING ME HAS been the best touch. Loving me has been the greatest ease. Loving me has been significant, to hold my hands, to see my face, to feel my worth inside of me. I am gone, Satan—whether you see it or not, I'm so far away from you. My essence will be no more. My touch you never felt, will come with a strength that you have never seen. My shine will be dull to you, because you won't be able to see when it comes. My lips will look like chalk from the words that will come out to bind you back into the pits of hell where you come from. My feet will look like elephant feet, because I will be able to trample all your imps that come around me. My eyes will look like the darkest day, because I will be able to see through the tunnels of the dark fabrications of the lies you tell. My life will be such a pain to the demons of darkness that held on to such a one like myself, and we will rain, with Jesus Christ, on your parade. This is why I say that loving me is the best thing I have done—I have given myself back the key to my life by accepting Jesus Christ in my life, who has forgiven me for all my sins and brought me out of your hands and back into the one that is called "I Am."

Amen, and amen.

# UPSIDE DOWN

UPSIDE DOWN I write this page; upside down is what I see. I feel the anguish and hurt that have slipped the upper side of me—a life that I say no more, downsizing for me, only for the one who has played the upper hand in my life, the one who helped turn my life upside down: Satan himself, who brought a vision of pain that tried to pin me down, backward in a confused and mixed-up world, with me not knowing who I was. He had a chance to get in through the back door that I left open, because of loving something that was not God. I loved a demon that hid himself in a man, who betrayed and influenced my every step, who knew how to use the tool that welcomed him, and I allowed it because I wanted to prove my worth to a man instead of to God. I don't blame anyone but myself. So upside down is why I write this page, because upside down is where I was.

Amen, and amen.

# MILLION DOLLAR BABY

I AM TALKING to a million dollar baby, and she doesn't even see the wealth and prosperity that have been handed to her by the one and only gift-giver of all that holds the key to her gifts, which have no limit. What she holds inside her is the life that will change the lives of people who need help in their destination, who need a way of escape. She holds life for sisters and brothers that belong to the most high Himself. People will shed a tear of gladness, of joy too great to comprehend, but it's called life, and the key to the kingdom.

Satan will ride her the best he knows, but she has learned to withstand the fire like Shadrach, Meshach, and Abednego who stood in the fiery furnace believing and knowing they had nothing to fear, because the only begotten Son, Jesus Christ, who stood beside them—she knows that she has His presence as well. She has a way of giving laughter to one who has lost their smile. She glows with the very essence of power that can make an old woman feel young, and an old man stand tall. The young will cling to her, just knowing they can be what God has made them to be: strong and courageous, loving life in better ways. Her love outshines the greatest gift, which comes only from the greater gift of Jesus. She will cling to His unchanging love. She will not falter by the wayside. She shall live in Him 100%, knowing that if there is a storm, she shall notice right away and ask for forgiveness not looking or slacking in knowing that isn't right. "Correction" shall be her name, changing the face for the believer who should and wouldn't, because of fear of doing what is entirely right. It is only the white robes that will enter in; God says no stains will enter through those pearly gates, so she has to go and get her white robes.

Amen, and amen.

# STOP SLEEPING

I WANTED TO go to church but there was none open for me to go in, so I went back home and started writing this note, about whether I could not have Christ in me, and not know it. Today I would have been put back into the wolves' den of depression without a notice, because it was hard just to leave the house. As the devil was attacking me with his hit list of depression, thank God I got the Word in me. What about the ones who don't? A re we going to sleep in this war, or be girded up to stand for the lost, and be ready for somebody? It doesn't matter if its choir rehearsal or a dance, somebody needs to be there. The time is at hand, and we don't have time to sleep anymore. Satan isn't asleep, and neither are his demons. They are trying to take down as many as they can. Christians, let's do it by the clock; let's take turns at the door. In Mark 14:34, Jesus asked His disciples to stay up with Him, but they went to sleep. If Jesus had not known the Word, He would have fallen into temptation when Satan talked to him. He was hungry, tired, and broke, like a lot of us, but Jesus used the Word. You see, I have the Word, too—do you? We need to act like it, and put it into perspective for the sake of the lost. This Christian life we live isn't a joke; we need each other. Satan got his, and we need ours to stand up and not be half and half. Some Christians are staying in lack, but we should all be whole in Jesus and remove all manifestations that keep each other down: jealousy, malice, covetousness. I'm talking about things that you do not want in your life, especially when you are trying to live for God. Those who have experienced this know what I am talking about. So let's turn it around, for the good of the kingdom; we are all lost sheep trying to find our way. So today, tell someone "God loves you," instead of asking "How are you?" Give the love that the kingdom is searching for—and that's the love of God. Jesus did it for us when He was humiliated on the cross for our sins. Let's give back, okay?

Amen, and amen.

I HOPE THAT in this testimony, you were able to see how I loved Bowlegs above everything: my kids, my family, myself, and my God. I actually made him my god, because I wanted him to be happy. It didn't matter what happened to me, even though I loved my kids. Satan had a hold on my life to the point that Bowlegs was my water, my food, and my air. Satan made me feel like he was the one I was supposed to serve. He made the darkness feel like Bowlegs was my light when I couldn't see. Satan crippled me in a major way, and he started when I was just a little girl looking for attention. My attention should have been on God, and only on Him, because I knew the Word. Many times, God had shown me Himself, but I acted like the Israelites, the chosen people, and got hard-headed and stiff-necked. I thank God that He gave me another chance to get it right, because of all the pain I placed on His children. He should have given up on me—those children were only babies, with no understanding of this life, and I treated them as if they were not human, because I gave in to Satan's ways of loving a man too much, rather than loving the ones who treated me right and fair, which were my children.

Today I say to my kids: I apologize for the insecurities I carried inside of me, not knowing when I should have known better, and the many times I did this. I thank You, Father, for giving me Your only Son, Jesus, so that I might have a right to the tree of life, and for giving me a way of escape so I can praise You with the Holy Spirit. And I say thank you to my mother, who stood behind me. Through thick and thin, thank you for being there for my children and me. To my sisters, thank you for the encouraging words that lifted me when I couldn't see at times. I thank my daughter-in-law, Duchess—baby girl, you stayed strong for my son when I know there were crying times and the pain of knowing that his mother had gone back out. Thank you to my sons-in-law, who were there for my daughters when they needed you, and to my nephews and nieces. To the love of my heart, Bobby—you kept me in times when I did not know what to do; you held me up and gave me strength by keeping God in our conversation and directing me so I would not have to go do the things I hated to do. Thank you so much. And to my brother James—thank you for your home, where you let me live and do whatever I wanted, without telling me to leave. I know you were tired of it, but you did that for me. Thank you Mama Carolyn, my mother-in-law; you talked to me, and you and Sunny gave me words of encouragement every Saturday, or whenever I would call. You never put me down. Thank you for loving me the right way, through Jehovah God who keeps us. To my girl Sharlet, thank you—when I needed someone's shoulder to cry on, you were there, not to tell me anything but to be strong, and I cried on your shoulder so many times. Believe me, when things were going on around me, I just needed you to be there. Thanks to Bill for my computer and phone that you purchased for me to get through all this. Trishall, Darrin, Jamela, Dashanieck, Shana, Dishan, and Desiree, I love you all, and thank you so much for being there for each other when I couldn't be there for you guys. Thank you for loving me even though times were hard. Thank you, and I love you all. To my sister in Christ, Mother Wiley, thank you for opening up your home to me when I had no food to eat, and thank you to the pastor for helping me with my ticket, and to the rest who gave me a bed to sleep in when my days were dark—I thank you all as well. I thank all my prayer warriors out there who prayed for me—you know who you are; there are too many to name. I can tell you guys that prayers lord—I made it. And to Bowlegs...I know you will read this book, and it is not meant to make you feel bad, but it is meant for God's children to understand that when we push God to the side, nothing good is going to happen. I say may God bless your days, and may you try to find Him, so that whoever God brings into your life, you can offer them Jesus. I ask you to forgive me for being me. God blesses all of you, so be encouraged.

Amen, and amen.

THE END

# The Testimony

MY TESTIMONY IS for those who think they cannot make it out, and who are in love with someone or something that has total control over their life, and they cannot see their way out. I have a message for them: Yes, you can call it out and claim change over your life, and claim tiredness over your life. When I say "claim," I'm talking about saying it out loud so the devil can hear it, and you can believe it for yourself. This testimony is for those who are tired of being abused by things they have brought into their lives. God gives grace, and He sustains the upright of heart. He hear that we are trying to get there, and He will bring you out, as long as you try to come out. I am a living witness: I walked out, and every day I prayed and I asked God to help me, and He did. He delivered me, and I am free because the Blood of Jesus set me free. Once I asked God to forgive me, and I forgave myself, that was when my change came. Now I am able to look to the hills, from which come my strength. So I say to you: Backslider, hold your head up, and don't give up—get out, because His mercy is new every day, and He is there, even when you think He is not.

Amen, and amen!

# Children of God

CHILDREN OF GOD, quit allowing the enemy to tell you that you are not worth it, that you are weak. Don't let the enemy criticize you by telling you "You're not all there yet." Who is all there? Nobody is, but I'm here to tell you that you are good enough. Believe that you have made it out, believe that you have made it through, believe that you are strong, believe that you know the Word of God, believe that God has brought you out, and believe that you are forgiven.

# HALF/HALF

WHAT IS HALF and half? Half and half is when you are trying to live two separate lives: a life of Christ, and a life of Satan. The Bible says God is a jealous God, and to enter into the Kingdom you must choose this day whom you are going to serve, because we cannot be hot and cold--there is no both; there is only one or the other, because unless we choose, God isn't a half God, where things are half done; everything he does is done all the way, not halfway. He says, "My Word will not return to me void," and I have learned that I can't serve both man and God, because when I gave all my heart, mind, and soul away to man, I didn't gain respect; it gave me only darkness. Now that I have given my heart and mind back to the One who gave them to me, I am living a wholehearted life that lets me see the light.

Amen, and amen.

# WHAT IS THE KINGDOM OF EVIL?

THE KINGDOM OF evil is demonic spirits that have entered into a person because the person themselves has allowed the spirits in. An evil spirit enters in, invited by the person who has allowed it, and has given an open invitation to demonic evil by living a life of sin. The Bible says in Ephesians 6:12, "For we wrestle not against flesh and blood, but against principalities, against powers, against the rulers of the darkness of this world, against spiritual wickedness in high places." We invite them by being hard-headed against God, being disobedient to what is right. Instead of lying and cheating and stealing from one another, we must put love in place of tall that, and then we will not allow the evil spirits in our minds, because that is where they start—in our minds. It starts with a thought that will damage the whole body by allowing you to have o peace and no joy, and it takes your hope away. So I say to you, put on the whole armor of God, that you may be able to withstand the evil day, and stand therefore, having your loins girt about with truth, and having on the breastplate of righteousness, and your feet shod with the preparation of the gospel of peace—and above all, taking the shield of faith, wherewith you shall be able to quench all the fiery darts of the wicked one. And remember, pray always with supplication. (Ephesians 6:13-18)

Amen, and amen.

# THE TOKEN

- I want to be able to give back to my neighborhood. While I was out there, I saw a lot of children who had nothing to do. School was out, and all they did was hang around on the street corners. Some tried to sell drugs, but they didn't have enough money to keep it up, and then they would give credit and wouldn't get their money back, so they wound up stealing and carrying guns, trying to take over spots, but that was not going to happen because the OGs had that all sold up. My desire is to give people something positive in their lives.

- I want to create a women's home, and help women who are lost? It's because I was once lost out there in the streets, wanting some positive feedback about how to change, but all I got was "You need to get out of the streets." But they couldn't show me how. I would say, "Yes, I know God, but God isn't going to come out of the sky and change me—I must be taught how. Show me." I had no idea how to really change, even though I had been down this road many times, and had tries to change. I had some strong-willed people in my life who stuck by me and gave me hope, and that's what I want to give back to my community, as well as to women and children in need, because there were many days when I would hear people say they were tired of the way they were living...and I mean young and old people alike. But as I looked around, what was available for them? Even the churches I saw were in need because people have been hurt so many times by all kinds of authority figures; they can't trust anyone. Right

112

now, we must build trust in our communities. It's not a black thing or a white thing—it's a people thing. We must build a community of real, God-fearing people out here in the world, looking for a positive outlook on life. And I want to give back to the community what God gave to me: another chance to get it right.

- I have been around to see the ugliness and evil out there. I have seen the hurting community that lacks communication with one another. I have seen homes break apart because of lack of knowledge, and people who are afraid to speak up or share or take a stand, because they fear nobody will hear their cry. I have seven children, plus another who is my stepson, and they have all been through a lot, as have my fifteen grandchildren. But now my entire family looks up to me as a source of strength, and I have met true friends who love and respect me for who I am.

- I have been on every drug you can name, except for heroin. I have walked the streets of prostitution. I have had my children taken from me due to my destructive lifestyle. I have seen prison walls, and have been around suffering, including those who feel there is no hope. Deep down inside, we are all lost, without direction in this world, especially when we have trust issues. So, what makes me qualified? Jesus, who died for all that I have seen and been through—He changed my life by giving me another chance. I was born with a vision that God has given me, and I want to step up and give it back. I want to give back knowledge and understanding of His people who suffer in violence, and who the enemy takes by force. I'm not alone in this—I have family ready to step in and help with the groundwork. I have a plan—so...what do you think? If you think this is a good idea, help me get started by sharing my story with others, and purchasing my book. Your help lets me go on sharing the vision, and making it a reality. I want to start where I am in Fresno, California, and then take it all over the nation, with the willing help of those who share my calling. And thank you.

Thank you so
much for the
Love you give to
me and I
pray you
enjoy
Every word
Deane Hall
1-30-14

This is your Season
to be blessed!
Dr. LaVonne Johnson
2014

Carmen

CPSIA information can be obtained at www.ICGtesting.com
Printed in the USA
LVOW08s0236311213

367548LV00001B/63/P

9 781478 724643

Johnson!